# MEMORY PALACE

**WILBUR CYRIL HALE**

# CONTENTS

# INTRODUCTION

A memory palace, also known as a mind palace, is a potent remembering technique that combines visuals with spatial memory. It's also known as the loci method, and it's the earliest way for remembering any piece of knowledge, reaching back to ancient Rome and Greece.

A memory palace is created by creating a path through a place that you are particularly familiar with. It's better if you know all there is to know about it. Then you choose things along the path to serve as anchor points. You'll need to practice this for a while before you can utilize it. Your path, the things, and their sequence must all be well-established in your mind. This is made easier by the fact that it is a location you are quite familiar with. You may start attaching various components to each thing along the way once you've fixed your path in your mind. The more outlandish the relationship, the more likely you are to recall it afterward. The goal is to weave a narrative out of the events that occur along your trip.

This book will explain why you should construct one, how to accomplish it, and what problems you should be aware of. To put it another way, it will show you how to construct your own Versailles.

The Memory Palace method is based on the notion that we're quite good at remembering places we've been before. A 'Memory Palace' is a metaphor for any well-known location that can be visualized simply. It may be the inside of your house or the route you go to work every day. That comfortable spot will serve as your guide for storing and recalling any type of knowledge. Let's have a look at how it works.

## A QUICK HISTORY

When the Greek poet and Sophos (wise man) Simonides identified imagery's profound memory powers, it seems to have garnered academic attention for the first time (c.556-c.468 B.C.E.). According to a narrative given down by Cicero (106-43 B.C.E. ), Simonides discovered while attending a dinner in Thessaly to offer a lyric song composed in favor of the host. Shortly after his performance, Simonides was summoned outside. While he was gone, the ceiling of the banqueting hall collapsed, crushing the other guests and mutilating several of their bodies beyond recognition. On the other hand, Simonides discovered that he could identify the dead (which was necessary for appropriate burial) by checking his visual memory image of the persons seated around the banqueting table, which allowed him to identify the dead according to where they were discovered. As a result of this encounter,

Persons desiring to train this faculty [of memory] must select places and form mental images of the things they wish to remember and store those images in the places so that the order of the places will preserve the order of the things, and the images of the things will denote the things themselves, and we will use the places and images respectively as a wax writing-down device. (Sutton & Rackham, 1942, translation of Cicero's De Oratore, II, lxxxvi).

This is thought to be the genesis of the mnemonic technique known as the method of loci, which was documented by Roman rhetoricians such as Cicero and Quintilian (c.35-c.95 C.E.) and was widely used by orators and others in different versions from classical through medieval to early modern periods. Indeed, it has been argued that this now-largely forgotten technique had a significant impact on the development of the Western intellectual tradition during the ancient, medieval, and Renaissance periods (Yates, 1966; Spence, 1985; Carruthers, 1990, 1998; Small, 1997; Rossi, 2000); for one thing, it helped to keep imagery at the forefront of cognition thinking during these periods (Yates, 1966; Spence, 1985; Carruthers, 1990, 1998; Small, 1997; Rossi, 2000). Although analogous imagery-based approaches would eventually come to be utilized for other objectives, such as spiritual exercises, the method of loci was initially employed by orators to recall the points to be presented in a speech in their right order. In one of the method's simplest iterations, the orator would memorize the layout of a complicated but familiar architectural area (such as the inside of a temple) so that he or she could clearly picture its many areas and characteristics. He'd then see things depicting the points to be remembered (for example, a sword to signify warfare) being placed at various loci (strategic landmark sites, such as the temple's niches and windows) around the room. The points may then be recalled in order while giving a speech by picturing going around the area along a set path, "seeing" the items by coming across them in their designated locations, and so being reminded, in order, of the points they indicated.

Very intricate versions of the process emerged in the Middle Ages and Renaissance, involving particularly taught imagined environments (Memory Theaters or Palaces) and intricate systems of prepared symbolic symbols, frequently imbued with occult or spiritual meaning. Modern experimental research has demonstrated that even a simple and readily taught variant of the loci method and various other imagery-based mnemonic strategies may be extremely efficient (Ross & Lawrence, 1968; Maguire et al., 2003).

# WHAT IS A MEMORY PALACE?

A memory palace is exactly what it sounds like. It's a mental place or region that you're quite familiar with and where you've accumulated a lot of information. On the other hand, the information does not float around aimlessly like a hazy recollection but is more accurately tied to numerous things or creatures inside the space itself. The size and number of palaces you may build are limitless. What is the reason behind this? Your imagination is their limit, and as you know, imagination knows no limitations. The palace might be real or imaginary, as long as you know your way around it like the back of your hand.

Visualization and spatial memory are the foundations of a memory palace. Visualization, also known as mental imagery, is the process of seeing objects, scenes, or events in your mind. In the absence of a direct and linked external stimulus, these representations are accompanied by sensory information. It's essentially "seeing with the mind's eye." The way the brain retains knowledge about the environment around you is referred to as spatial memory. These two ideas are a wonderful match, each contributing to the building of your memory palace in their own unique way. They essentially allow you to retrace your steps whenever you misplace your keys mentally, and they allow rats to navigate through a labyrinth in search of food or safety.

My house was my first memory palace. You can, of course, have several memory palaces. The premise is that you create a route and follow it, stopping at specific sites in the same order every time. Those places are known as loci, which is derived from the Latin locus, which means location. Your front door might be a very simple loci. The concept now is that you visualize a monatomic at those locations.

Any memory method that aids in remembering something is referred to as a mnemonic.

If you wish to learn the word freedom, envision a little replica of the Statue of Liberty standing in front of your front door. According to studies, our brain is awful at really learning something by merely reading words repeatedly. Because I have a psychology background, I believe this is extremely probable because our brain evolved thousands of years before written language existed. So, to learn successfully, we must convert knowledge into a format that our brain can understand.

# WHY RULE A MEMORY PALACE?

When confronted with anatomical listings, your first instinct is to make a mnemonic out of them. This strategy will almost surely provide positive outcomes, but why not aim for the best? Mnemonics are learned by rehearsing them. On the other hand, memory palaces can help you take your learning to the next level, especially if your anatomy department's instruction is regional. The following are some of the extra and appealing qualities of mind palaces:

- **Perfect for anatomy** - Drilling information into your brain is the focus of anatomy. All of those artery and nerve branchings, trajectories, and muscle facts need a minimum of comprehension but a maximum of memorizing. Furthermore, several elements must be mastered in a precise order. Fortunately, memory palaces are explicitly designed for this learning style, so they will undoubtedly assist you with this subject!

- **They work!** - The strength and benefits of the loci technique have been demonstrated by a body of research studies. At least 85% of the students who took part in the studies thought this learning technique was really beneficial and agreed to utilize it again in the future. In comparison to mnemonics or rehearsal-based strategies, their long-term memory was greatly enhanced.

- **Meditative** - There's no denying that learning anatomy is difficult. Not to add the tension that comes with exams and the psychological demands of regular life! Surprisingly, memory palaces can assist you in resolving such issues. Scientific research has shown that developing an emotional memory palace might help persons with depression cope better with their symptoms. They don't fill it with anatomical information; instead, they fill it with positive ideas, sensations, and prior events that make them grin. You may also construct a palace like this to unwind and enhance your mood. It's the ideal way to get rid of those anxieties before examinations!

- **Infinitely creative** - A memory palace does not have to be a physical location. It may be anything you want it to be, as long as you know it by heart. As a result, just let your mind go wild and construct it the way you like, particularly in terms of visuals and connotations. The funnier and more ludicrous they are, the easier they will stick in your mind.

## HOW TO BUILD YOUR PALACE?

Your memory palace requires a solid foundation and a crystal clear design to endure all of the everyday distractions and continual mental encoding. The last thing you need is to get lost inside it during those few hours of your anatomy test!

*The stages to creating a masterpiece to rival Versailles are as follows:*

**Step 1:** Make a mental note of the details you need to recall. Let's pretend today's menu item is Kenhub's essay about the axillary artery and its branches.

**Step 2:** Consider a familiar environment you may describe in your dream, such as your bedroom. Spend a few moments visualizing every facet of it in as much detail as you can. Choose a direction, such as clockwise, then mentally describe everything in the room as you travel around the room. Concentrate on the small things, such as colors, patterns, size, texture, odors, generated emotions, and so on. If you've run out of well-known locales, construct your own and publicize it!

**Step 3:** The principle of visualizing is the focus of this stage. Take all of the items on your list and try to make a picture out of them. Because many anatomical terms are abstract, you'll need to practice this procedure because you'll utilize it virtually every time. The superior thoracic artery, the first branch on the list, can be seen as a flying thoracic cage clad in Superman's suit in this example. Alternatively, imagine Thor, the fictional figure, downing a large bowl of soup. Make your photos as exaggerated and humorous as possible, and you will not soon forget them! In addition, competent educators understand the importance of images and connections. Be grateful if your instructor starts telling you humorous anecdotes and making parallels throughout your anatomy classes; he or she is on to something!

**Step 4:** You're now ready to combine visuals with spatial memory. Consider your chosen location and the first thing in it, together with all of the associated data. Let's pretend this is the entrance to your bedroom. You must now mentally correlate the image of the superior thoracic artery with the image of the door. You may imagine the thoracic cage dressed as Superman as the door handle flying around erratically above the entrance, making it impossible to hold and enter. The second alternative is to imagine Thor, who is currently consuming the large bowl of soup, literally occupying the entire door frame, forcing you to crawl inside your bedroom. Continue in your selected, clockwise orientation, linking each image on your list with the next object within your bedroom until you reach the finish.

**Step 5:** Continue to revise by going through your memory palace on a regular basis. However, don't do it at random, especially at first. Instead, keep continuing in the same direction, repeating the same actions, and envisioning the same stuff. It will become so deeply embedded after a period that you will be able to recall the knowledge upside-down and backward!

Despite the seemingly unlimited choices (rooms, houses, schools, voyages, cities, artifacts, and so on), you may have exhausted all of your well-known locales or lack the will to construct one. So, what exactly do you do? You don't give up easily! Instead, start utilizing 'nested locations.' Zooming in on a certain object or area inside your selected space is comparable to this. Focus on the intricacies and elements displayed inside each picture, building "nests" of knowledge, for example, if your memory palace is your favorite art gallery with fifty photographs on display. As you can see, you've just increased the number of possible associations from fifty to hundreds, if not thousands. You can even subdivide a large space into many smaller, more detailed spaces, resulting in a multitude of palaces from a single concept.

# TYPES OF MEMORY PALACES

## 1. The Bird's-eye/3rd Person Memory Palace

This type of Memory Palace entails seeing down through a building's roof. It's as though you're looking at a floor plan.

This stage is critical because it teaches your brain to think about space in a new way, which aids in the development of your mental rotation skills.

The procedure is straightforward:

- Select a location suited to creating a Memory Palace (usually a familiar building, but parks and other locations will do)
- Get out a sheet of paper, ideally in a Memory Journal devoted to Memory Palace creation.
- Draw the Memory Palace.
- Strategically structure your course through the Memory Palace.
- Practice it mentally.
- Use it to memorize something by drawing upon the tools of Magnetic Association

If you're stumped as to where to look, How to Find Memory

Palaces will assist.

These elaborative encoding activities can be helpful if you need assistance constructing the images.

## 2. The 2nd Person Memory Palace

You or a Bridging Figure navigate through your Memory Palace as though via the lens of an external camera in this type of Memory Palace.

This is not a substitute for sketching Memory Palaces but rather a new method of thinking about and experiencing the navigation process.

## 3. The 1st Person Memory Palace

Here's what happens when you use a Memory Palace like this:

You envision yourself within the Memory Palace. After that, you picture yourself viewing the adventure through your own eyes.

You may also pretend to be a character in a video game, series, or film and see the world through their eyes.

For example, I might picture myself as this Giordano Bruno monument and observe portions of Rome I've made as Memory Palace via his eyes utilizing an outdoor Memory Palace.

## 4. The Virtual Memory Palace

Virtual Memory Palaces exist in all Memory Palaces to some extent.

What is the reason behind this? You're inventing a fictional concept. This structure is based on a real-life structure or location. In your mind's eye, you're navigating it "virtually."

However, building a Memory Palace in a location you've personally visited reduces cognitive stress significantly.

Consider the following scenario:

Did you have to work hard to recall the layout when you last moved into a new home?

Most likely not. That's what makes recalling it so simple.

However, when utilizing a video game as a Memory Palace, you must not simply uniquely memorize the layout.

Because you've never been there, you'll have to re-create the layout using greater mental resources.


## 5. The Magnetic Memory Palace

This type of Memory Palace allows you to combine all four

ways into a single Memory Palace plan.

Memory exercise feels a lot like a Memory Palace game with Recall Rehearsal!

When you apply the Magnetic Memory Method tools, you can actually....

- Sea shelling
- The Pillar Technique
- Ample use of Magnetic Bridging Figures
- Recall Rehearsal
- The Big 5 of Learning (Also called the levels of processing)

Everything becomes a lot simpler. This is because it gets more enjoyable.

Not only that, but when utilized as a part of a comprehensive Memory Palace Network, the Magnetic Memory Palace also makes Recall Rehearsal faster and easier.

(Recall Rehearsal is a short and enjoyable "memory game" for swiftly storing any knowledge in long-term memory.)

As an added benefit, you can convert your Memory Palaces to Mind Maps and vice versa. These examples of mind mapping will teach you how.

This may not be the case for everyone.

Virtual Memory Palaces, on the other hand, I believe will cost most of us more time and energy than they are worth.

# VIRTUAL REALITY MEMORY PALACES

For thousands of years, the ancient mnemonic "Method of Loci" has been in use. The strategy, which combines visual and spatial clues, helps pupils and memory competitors memorize objects. Many people may be familiar with the approach because of famous TV programs like Sherlock or Hannibal. In these characters, ' "Mind Palaces" or "Memory Palaces" are depicted as a brilliant character. The genuine approach, on the other hand, is dead easy. It's much easier if you have a virtual reality headset.

But, before we get into how we may make our own Memory Palaces (or Mind Palaces) in VR, let's define what a Memory Palace is. You'll need a physical or virtual place to carry out the procedure. It should be a familiar location, such as your apartment or a setting from your favorite video game. You then isolate the number of rooms and sub-parts of those rooms that total the number of items you wish to remember. After that, you might want to create a mental walkthrough of your Memory Palace. This is where the approach comes into play: you visualize what you wish to remember in the Mind Palace's designated locations. Do you have to go shopping? Consider coffee grounds strewn on the floor, orange juice boxes were strewn on the sofa, and bananas dangling from the television. If you need to remember something more abstract, become creative and utilize the visualization to link to the information you need to remember.

*"Get out of here; I have to get to my Mind Palace."* In the BBC's *Sherlock, Benedict Cumberbatch is rather busy in his Memory Palace. edthatch created this illustration.*

This strategy is thought to be effective because of the coupling of information with visual cues (representing memory elements) and spatial cues (their given place in the environment). Surprisingly, this exploitation of visual and spatial cues in the brain does not require our eyesight or genuine perception of three-dimensional spatial locations at all — instead, it relies on our "inner eye" and our previously-stored spatial memories. However, virtual reality (VR) has the potential to change this. Instead of viewing the Memory Palace as only a mental construct, we might immerse ourselves in it, making it both exterior and internal.

Adapting the Memory Palace methodology to the medium of Immersive Virtual Reality is thus an ideal undertaking. We may practice this procedure with raw, fresh vision in VR, which provides us with both the visual and spatial parts of our Memory Palace. We are given a highly optimizable visuospatial environment created of software in VR, which allows us to customize the Memory Palaces to our own needs. The approach may function even better or be more enjoyable and easier to use if the visuospatial parts of the Method of Loci are exploited in a much more clear sense.

# STEPS TO BUILD AND USE THE MEMORY PALACE

Let's imagine you're planning a little get-together at a friend's place. You get in your car and go over, but you need to locate a parking spot. Because his block is congested, you'll have to park one block away. After that, you enter the house and need to hang your keys. You place them on his living room's coffee table.

After a few more people arrive and some time has passed, you notice that it's becoming warm, so you remove your jacket and toss it over the chair. The celebration has come to a conclusion, and everyone has had a terrific time. It's time to go, but how are you going to know where everything is? You're well aware that you must depart with your jacket, keys, and, of course, your automobile. What is the reason behind this? They are permanent goods for you because you brought them with you.

You know where your jacket is - it's slung over the chair. Then you see your keys as you go out and remember that you have to park a street away.

The process of exiting that gathering is remarkably similar to what you would experience in a mind palace. You see items you know you need, such as your coat, keys, and automobile, and they remind you of other things, such as where you put them.

With that in mind, here are five easy steps to make and use your own functioning mind palace.

# 1) Decide on the map's location

The arrangement of your mental palace is critical to its proper functioning.

While it is possible to create your layout entirely from your ideas, this will require time and energy that you do not have. The idea is to get so comfortable with the layout of your castle that you can mentally walk around it without thinking about it.

In truth, the human memory system is designed to be associative. This implies that we save data according to the context in which it is used. Elaborative Encoding is how we use a mind palace to encode short-term information into long-term memory, and it works by linking one memory to previous memories. Every memory is linked to another memory. It is simpler to recollect it if it has a lot of attachments.

With this in mind, the following are some of the top places to visit:

- Your house
- Your workplace
- Your school
- A childhood park

Any area you're familiar with is the finest potential site for a mental palace.

On a side note, we now have a new alternative that did not exist previously with the relatively recent advent of video games. Maps and locales from video games may also be used to create mind palace layouts. After traversing so many circles, the Zombies theater layout in Black Ops, for example, is indelibly etched in my mind.

You're ready to start adding details once you've set the location of your palace and memorized it completely.

## 2) ESTABLISH THE MAIN ITEMS

Now, provided you can mentally stroll through the palace without losing track of specifics, you're ready to begin assigning permanent things.

In each room, you should choose 4-5 objects. The following are the best choices:

- Furniture
- Artwork
- Windows
- Decorations
- Other prominent features.

In each room, try to avoid picking two of the same thing. For example, if you have a dining area, do not utilize each individual chair as a distinct item. Instead, treat the entire collection as if it were a single piece. When you add knowledge, this will keep your brain from being confused.

To give you an idea of what I'm talking about, the first room in my mental palace (my living room) has a rocking rocker in the corner, a sofa next to it, and a tall standing lamp. A love seat, a fireplace, a bookcase, and some colorful wall art are also included. This is a highly complex room with various things, but it's not too difficult to recall because the outline is already stored in my long-term memory. It also helps that the objects are distinct enough that I have no difficulty distinguishing them.

You're ready to go on to the next phase in the procedure once you've mastered this phase.

## 3) DETERMINE YOUR ROUTE

The majority of individuals are taken aback by this action. In other words, you must arrange everything in your chamber and stick to it every time you utilize your mental palace.

When I first heard about the mind palace approach, I imagined myself wandering aimlessly about my palace, finding things I wanted to remember. While this appears to be true in part, it misrepresents how a mind palace actually works.

The functioning of a mind palace is mostly dependent on repetition and visual cues. So now that you've memorized your mind palace and picked the stuff within it, you need to create a path that you'll always follow when recalling information. To put it another way, you must place your order. It may be simpler for some people to assign a number to each object in their memory palace.

For example, I always enter by my front door, then turn right and work my way counterclockwise around my house. I also work counterclockwise in each room till I reach the start of the trip.

You're ready to start adding information once you've identified a route through your mind palace and know it like the back of your hand. Self-testing is an easy approach to see whether you're ready. "Can you tell me what the third object in the second room is?" You're ready if you can think of it immediately without walking through all the rooms.

## 4) ADDING INFORMATION TO PERMANENT ITEMS

This is the part you've been waiting for: adding data to your mental castle. You must associate something with each object in each area now that we have a mental image of the rooms memorized.

It's important to remember that the mind palace is a visual memory method, so you'll need to put whatever information you wish to learn into a visual format. This implies converting numbers, cards, exam information, or a voice into visual information.

A few strategies have been developed to assist you in this

"conversion," but many individuals choose to accomplish it independently. Converting knowledge into an outrageous visually/sensory exciting picture is the initial stage in adding information.

This is aided by bright colors, strange textures, noises, sensations, and movement.

After you've completed this with your data, you can begin to distribute it around your palace following the path you've chosen. This is the point at which the route begins to serve as a valuable tool.

Assume you're memorizing a deck of cards, and the first card is a Hearts Ace. So, you'd identify the image you made for an Ace of Hearts with your first object in your first room. So the Ace of Hearts in my deck is represented by a monkey with a bright red bum going wild (it sounds nuts, but it's visually appealing and memorable).

My palace's first room is a little coat closet to the right of the main door. With that in mind, I enter my thought palace and peer into the little closet, where I discover a monkey with a bright red bum going insane... the Ace of Hearts.

Let's assume the next card you get is a Four of Spades. To me, a Four of Spades resembles a gleaming black party cone hat perched on a shovel (a spade is a type of shovel). The railing that divides the foyer from the living room is my next stop. After seeing the monkey in the closet, I glance next to it and find a gleaming black party hat placed on a spade poised on the railing...Four of Spades.

I'd keep doing this until I'd memorized the full deck of cards by placing them in the order I wanted them in my mind palace. Then, when I want to remember them, I return to my castle and look at the photographs in each location. For the card they represent, such visuals serve as a memory trigger.

Many different types of data can be used in this procedure. The recurrence of the same place and journey, as well as the visual/sensory images, are what make the palace so effective. However, when it comes to the mind palace, the majority of people are concerned.

"What if you've added some knowledge to your mind palace, and now you're trying to add more, and your brain is confused by the two lists of things?"

The solution is straightforward but not simple.

## 5) CREATE MORE THAN ONE

Yes, the solution is that straightforward. You're probably familiar with other locations across the world, so you can build additional palaces.

For many widely recalled themes, many memory champions will establish many palaces.

One will be dedicated to cards, one to numbers, one to lists, and one to speeches, for example. The problem is that you'll have to devote significantly more time and effort to creating and memorizing each palace.

You are correct if you think this seems like a lot of memory work only to construct the intended systems to assist you with your memory. This is why so many individuals fail to make appropriate use of the memory palace. They haven't spent enough time on it in advance to be able to use it successfully afterward.

You may now begin developing and using your mind palace by following these five steps (s).

It takes time and effort to get started using it to its maximum potential. Ease and speed will come with practice, and as you discover more strategies for tethering more information, recalling more complicated knowledge will become simpler.

Begin by building one palace and work your way up from there.

**Final Thoughts**

The more we become older, the more crucial memory retention becomes. We risk exposing ourselves to greater and more hassles if we do not train our intellect.

Make it a practice to grow your intellect, just as you would your body. The memory palace could be exactly what you're looking for to get started.

# How to Use Your Memory Palace

It's now time to learn how to put words and phrases on each of your Memory Palace's stations. We'll employ the three traditional principles of learning and memory to make these words and stations stick in your mind. These are the following:

- Paying attention in a special way to target words and phrases.

- Encoding the sound and meaning of information using imagery and action so each word or phrase becomes memorable.

- Decoding imagery and actions so you can move words and phrases into long-term memory.

Create visuals that are huge, brilliant, colorful, strange, and loaded with tremendous activity to encode your information. You may save the photographs to a Memory Palace station and return to them at any time.

Tip: Make this vision exaggerated enough that you can recall it using sounds and meaning.

For instance, if you're studying Spanish and discover that "Tengo por dar y regalar" roughly translates to "I've got lots to share," would you remember that phrase right away?

Probably not.

But what if I told you I witnessed a bizarre tango dance with Darth Vader tangled in a parachute? He tries to share an egg with his dance partner in irritation by trilling an "r" with his tongue through his breathing grill. She is a gigantic egg who gets tied up in the parachute with Darth Vader. "No thanks, I have plenty," she says. "No, really," Darth Vader says, "I've got enough to share."

Do you have a mental image of the scene? Because it's such a unique image, there's a good possibility you can.

Consider how this situation would play out in your bathtub. Concentrate solely on the essentials. When you return your thoughts back to your bathroom tub and decode it, you need this type of bizarre visual and sound-based tale.

*Here's the formula:*

Tango + para(chute) + Dar(th Vader) trilling "r" and handing off an r"eggular"ular = "tengo para dar y regalar."

The phrase will swiftly pour itself into long-term memory after a few returns to the tale and practice decoding it for sound and meaning, followed by use in a speaking session.

Take note of how I've used visuals and gestures to connect sound to meaning in this example. It's not simply that Darth Vader is trilling his "r" and passing an egg around aids in recalling the word's sound. The action also aids in the regularization of the word's meaning in the context of the sentence.

There is no one-to-one correlation in this scenario. I haven't yet included "y," but if I do, it'll be as simple as having Darth Vader wear a "y" shaped neck brace and yell "eee" at the scenario. However, if you let little words like "y" take care of themselves, they will.. Suppose you're ready to trust your memory after training it using these tactics. In that case, you'll be pleasantly surprised by how well it functions, as memory champion Ben Pridmore once stated in an interview. Similar situations and visuals may be created on your own, and they'll be near enough to trigger your memory. The more you practice, the more proficient you will become.

And keep in mind that these are just mnemonic examples from my head. You must create your own pictures and actions for these methods to function for you.

This narrative appeals to me since I am a Star Wars fan, I enjoy tango music, and it is just the image that my brain conjured up. The crucial idea to remember here is that the more you rely on knowledge already stored in your memory, the less effort you'll have to put in to learn new things. And if you relax and allow your imagination to go wild, you'll discover that with just a little effort, you, too, can generate memorable and helpful pictures like these.

# Enter Abraham Lincoln!

We can go even farther and utilize a bridge figure to make the combination of a Memory Palace station and a bathtub considerably more beneficial.

A bridging figure is a notion that can help you supercharge your Memory Palace and learn faster. This character is a fictional character who travels through your Palace and interacts with your photos for each phrase. Your bridging figure should ideally be someone you recognize.

For example, I use Abraham Lincoln to represent words that begin with the letter "A."

You can see Abraham Lincoln help me memorize four Spanish words via a journey at my old Berlin workplace in this example.

Bed – Abajo: Abraham Lincoln smashing to" ba" cco into a banjo "down below" his feet.

Desk – Abrir: Abraham Lincoln tearing a hole in the "rear" of his pants to reveal an "ear."

Wall – Abuela: Abraham Lincoln says "boo" in Grandma Ella Fitzgerald's ear. My Grandpa shouts "lo" (Abuelo) and pulls Ella away. She says," Los" as they pair up (abuelos).

# PRACTICAL TIPS FOR USING YOUR MEMORY PALACE TO MASTER A FOREIGN LANGUAGE

A Memory Palace is an effective language learning tool that may be used in conjunction with other methods to help you learn and speak a foreign language.

It just takes a few hours to create a Memory Palace, and as you get better at it, this style of learning will help you expand your vocabulary faster.

Draw on your Memory Palace frequently as part of your speaking practice once you've stored words and phrases inside. You could stumble and halt when looking up these terms and phrases, but don't worry: we all do it in our language.

The words and pictures you've generated in your Memory Palace will come back to you when you need them if you practice and relax, and they'll make learning and speaking a foreign language feel easier and more fun. So, if you're ready to start building a Memory Palace and utilizing it to memorize words and phrases, you may start tapping your memory for familiar locales right now. Good luck with your memorization!

1. Using the ideas you've just studied, design a well-constructed Memory Palace.

2. Take it easy. When you're psychologically and physically stress-free, memory methods perform best.

3. Memorize a list of terms, preferably in alphabetical order.

4. Write down the terms, definitions, and mnemonics on paper or in an Excel file or something similar.

5. Look up the definitions of each term in your written record or Excel file, as well as any other sources that may lead you to cheat.

6. On a piece of paper, write down the terms and their meanings depending on your memory. If you miss a word or your associative picture fails to activate the sound and meaning of a word in your list, don't worry. This is something you can solve afterwards.

7. Compare your record to the list you made from memory.

8. Use these terms in discussions, write them down in a ten-sentence email, and look for them when you read and listen to your target language.

# TIPS AND TRICKS FOR LANGUAGE LEARNING

Here are a few additional pointers to help you develop your memory palace for language learning.

- **Start with the obvious connections.**

If you're learning a language for the first time, you'll come across a lot of basic terminology for everyday situations. These will be the most straightforward to include in a memory palace. Place all food terms in the kitchen, clothes terms in the bedroom, and bathing terms in the bathroom. There's no reason to make things more complicated than they have to be.

After you've exhausted the obvious, let your imagination go wild. As previously said, it is much simpler to recall strange things, therefore make your castle strange. Remember that die Birne is the German term meaning "pear"? Consider a pear on fire in your kitchen. You might envision an extremely lengthy Wile E. Coyote giving a lecture in your living room to recall the word for "boring" is langweilig. Although these are very particular instances, the goal is to figure out what works best for you.

- **Make more than one memory palace.**

You probably know a lot about a lot of places in the globe, so once you've filled one up, go on to another. You may build a castle on your way to work or at a friend's house. If at all feasible, try to discover castles that are loosely related to the vocab you're attempting to learn.


- **Reuse your palaces.**

Memory palaces are reusable, which may seem illogical. Start cycling in new concepts and visuals if you feel like you have a decent handle on the language in one. You'll never run out of new palace design ideas this way.

# How To Memorize Vocab When Learning A New Language

## Choose Your Words Wisely

Focusing on relevant words to your life and hobbies can improve your ability to memorize them significantly. Not only will you be more likely to recall terms that interest you, but you'll also be reducing the vast number of words in your new language to a far more manageable quantity.

Luca Lampariello, an expert language learner, explained to Babbel why he feels word choice is so important:

It becomes much more challenging to locate new words to learn, let alone memorize, as your vocabulary in a language develops. During this stage, you must concentrate on helpful and relevant terms – terms that are relevant to your daily life, your profession, and your hobbies. This vocabulary is the foundation of what I refer to as personal fluency.

## Associate Freely And Often

Assigning significance to something is the greatest method to remember it. Words are essentially strings of characters without context, making them incredibly difficult to remember.

However, if you can link the term to something you already know or find intriguing, it will be far more likely to remain in your mind.

To assist provide this context, Lampariello suggests connecting multiple new words in a phrase. Use all of the terms in a phrase if you're learning the words for dog, cat, rain, and sun, for example. The cat, on the other hand, prefers rain over the sun. It might be true or false, but it'll almost surely help you remember the terminology!

## Set It In Stone (Or On Paper)

If you've ever attended a class in school, you've undoubtedly been advised that taking notes is the most effective approach to retain information. It will serve two functions to write down or record yourself reciting vocab terms and their meanings. To begin with, it will aid in the ingraining of the words in your mind, as your high school history instructor advised. Second, it will serve as a study guide that you may use to go over the terms you've previously mastered. When it comes to memorizing vocab in a new language, this is one of the most effective methods for ensuring that information sticks in your mind.

## Don't Stop Reviewing

Reviewing the content at frequent intervals is a crucial aspect of the learning process. Refreshing your memory through spaced repetition aids in the transfer of vocab from short-term to long-term memory. In fact, the Babbel Method for teaching languages includes this as a crucial component.

There are various excellent methods for reviewing vocabulary, both alone and with a companion. Making flashcards with the word on one side and the translation on the other, or better yet, writing a phrase with a few of the vocab words on one side and the entire phrase translation on the other is one solitary alternative. Teaching a buddy some of the terms you've learned and how to apply them in context is a more sociable choice.

The issue with new information or a new talent is that if you don't apply it, it fades away over time, leaving you back where you started on your learning path. Practice may not make perfect, but it will ensure that the content you've learnt is not forgotten.

Using new vocabulary terms in actual, meaningful discussions is the greatest method to reinforce them. To ensure that your new language is remembered, speak it with a study partner, an instructor, or a native speaker. There are few things more aggravating than losing information you've fought so hard to acquire.

# TRICKS FOR MEMORIZATION: WOW THEM WITH YOUR NEXT SPEECH

For others, giving a prepared public speech appears to be practically impossible. The Memory Palace approach, on the other hand, can be a useful tool for giving a focused and successful speech.

Have you ever been so nervous before giving a rehearsed speech that you almost pulled your hair out? If you have, don't feel awful. Giving a speech may be stressful.

The notion of giving a speech in front of an audience can cause some people to freeze up so completely that remembering a speech becomes impossible. There is, however, a remedy for everyone. Regardless of your level of expertise with prepared presentations in public, the first stage is to relax.

*There are various advantages to relaxing when preparing and memorizing a speech:*

- It opens up the critical thinking abilities of your mind.

- It stimulates the imagination.

- It conditions you to be relaxed during recall.

- It helps you set your audience at ease because you look and feel more confident.

- It helps you get back on track even if you lose your place.

For example, you could surprise yourself by eliciting laughter when you least expect it. This occurred during the TEDx Talk "Two Easily Recallable Questions That Silence Negative Thoughts." When the unexpected occurred, it was simple to get back on track, thanks to relaxing.

Try a five-minute meditation to help you unwind. You may also use breathing techniques to help you relax your muscles. Progressive muscle relaxation is a third approach that simply entails tensing and releasing all of your main muscles from head to toe. Combine all three tactics for the greatest results.

At each level of the speech preparation and delivery process, I propose that you prepare yourself to be calm. Establish a calm state before beginning to write your speech, relax before practicing, and repeat the procedure before presenting the speech.

Make an outline beforehand to help you remember things from

the start of the writing process. Then, using a pen or pencil, compose the speech on paper.

### Why write your speech by hand?

For example, in 59 Seconds, Richard Wiseman presents persuasive scientific evidence demonstrating that writing by hand engages more of your intellect. Long before it's time to memorize, you'll be tapping into the fertile ground of your memory.

It's now time to type your draft. This type of repetition not only helps you remember the speech but it also improves your memory. It also aids in the logical evolution of your ideas. The key to memorizing your speech with ease is to sequence your ideas so that they link and flow.

After that, deliver the speech aloud and videotape it. You'll activate the muscles of your lips by reading the address out, adding another layer of expression to the physical activities of handwriting and typing.

Then, while you read along with the text, listen to your speech again. You're now adding your ears to the work you've done with your hands, arms, eyes, and lips as another kind of repetition. These high degrees of repetition, along with the information's logical structure, will increase your familiarity even more.

Finally, segment the speech and make use of your body and surroundings. Creating a Memory Palace is one of the finest ways to make the most of your surroundings. This method of learning how to memorize a speech has been around since at least Ancient Greece. The English term "in the first place" relates to using locations to assist us to recall the points we wish to express.

## MEMORY PALACE CREATION 101

Here's a brief rundown if you've never used a Memory Palace before:

A Memory Palace is a fictitious recreation of a well-known real-world structure. A protected Memory Palace may be built at your home, at work, or even at an art museum or movie theater.

*Then, follow these procedures, remembering that, despite its complexity, this procedure should only take two to five minutes:*

1. Draw a floor plan of the location.

2. Number each room.

3. Make a list of each room beside the drawing (office kitchen, your office, secretary's office, boss's office, etc.):

4. Make a mental journey throughout the building.

Make the journey linear, logical and avoid crossing your path. Following these guidelines will reduce confusion and cognitive overload so you can focus on memorizing your speech.

5. Assign each segment of your speech to a room.

Now that you've got your Memory Palace prepared:

6. In your imagination, associate imagery with the ideas in your speech.

For example, you may see a magnifying glass concentrating beams of light from the sun onto a smaller representation of your workplace while memorizing a point about global warming and its consequences on your business. Imagine it erupting in flames on the kitchen counter of your office.

If the following point is about your company's $3 million plan to include solar energy into its future planning, imagine Donald Trump (a billionaire) putting the number "3" on a massive check in the shape of a solar panel. You could even give him a mustache to help you recall the number "3," as mustaches are fashioned like the number (tipped on its side).

Make sure the graphic is large, vivid, and colorful. It's much great if you can include some lively activity. Donald Trump, for example, maybe writing the check-in the same way that Zorro slashes his sword.

Learn how to memorize a textbook to augment this strategy if you've included more specific info.

7. As you memorize each portion of the speech, roam about the building you're utilizing as your Memory Palace if you can.

This will use your body's largest muscles, broadening your sensory experience for the benefit of your memory.

Again, the present custom of stating "first and foremost," "secondarily," "thirdly," and so on stems from how ancient Roman orators delivered speeches in Memory Palaces.]

These speakers were really visualizing the locations and visuals they utilized to memorize their talks in the logical order of their arguments and the Memory Palace's linear sequence. The key is to make sure your associations are definite, precise, and exaggerated.

8. By mentally strolling through the mental Memory Palace and "decoding" the visuals, you may practice giving your speech.

Do this three to five times.

You may also practice recall by walking around the area. Write down your speech from memory for bonus points and more practice.

All of these exercises should be completed in a relaxed attitude. It will make a significant impact and provide you with a stress-free edge when you deliver your speech. Nobody else will be as composed and composed as you.

Now is the moment to relax your thoughts. Sleep helps to solidify memories, so go to bed early.

Also, get up early. Eat a protein-rich breakfast and go through the speech with your Memory Palace a couple more times.

Then, with confidence, give your speech and congratulate yourself on your success.

Practice long-term memory to take it to the next level.

Give more speeches to improve your ability to deliver them from memory. To practice or speak at community events, you can join Toastmasters. There are multiple speeches about utilizing Memory Palaces on TedTalks, which is an excellent resource for watching presenters. For some ideas, look at this one by Joshua Foer.

Now it's your turn

Create a speech and remember it using the technique you just learned. Although it may appear to take a lot of effort, you'll be shocked at how quickly you can remember a multipage speech in one afternoon if you follow the procedures. Even if you don't have the luxury of sleeping in and practicing in the morning, you'll be astonished at how quickly you can learn and recall a full speech.

# HOW TO MASTER MEMORY IMPROVEMENT?

## THE FOUNDATION: ENERGY

You can't teach anything to a corpse, no matter how many memory tricks you apply. The brain needs oxygen and glucose to function at its most basic level. But, in a larger sense, anyone may enhance their brain's essential functioning by doing various activities. I strongly advise you to focus on your mental energy before diving into mnemonics and retention techniques.

You may take some very basic changes today that will have a MASSIVE impact on most people's mental concentration.

## THE MAGIC: MNEMONICS

It is natural for our brains to recall noteworthy things. Numbers, dates, and vocabulary terms aren't very memorable on their own. Making something memorable is the key to making it simpler to recall. Isn't that obvious?

The number 3594 is difficult to recall for most people. It isn't really noteworthy in and of itself. However, many athletes would associate that number with Roger Bannister's performance as the first human to run a mile in under four minutes (think about it: his time was 3:59.4, just 0.6 seconds short of 4 minutes).

Remembering numbers, phrases, and names is all about associating them with something other than themselves.

Anyone who is educated enough to talk and read may become very adept at remembering anything using these strategies with practice.

## KEEP IT: REVIEW

You'll have an easier time remembering material initially if you apply the correct energy and mnemonic methods to any memory assignment. However, it's critical to examine your material at least a few times, at proper intervals, to ensure that it stays with you permanently.

## TECHNIQUES

The three ideas outlined above have been used into a variety of memory approaches. Therefore, they may be classified into three groups:

**1. Image clues:** These are memory aids that use visuals to convey ideas.

Image hints, like logos or symbols, might prompt your brain to consider difficult concepts.

Memorable, multisensory visuals are paired or sequenced with others or placed in your "mind's eye" around familiar locations.

To "peg" fresh information onto ready-made photos, certain techniques have been created.

**2. Storytelling strategies:** These are technologies that make use of the fact that well-told stories are instantly remembered.

To recall lists, procedures, and all the points you wish to convey in essays or presentations, use storytelling tactics to link discrete visual cues into extended chains.

Choosing an environment that is related to your subject matter will help you remember more.

**3. Spatial systems:** These technologies allow you to save fresh knowledge using all of your previous real-world trips. These excursions may involve your commute to work or a favorite rural stroll.

You also know your way around a variety of structures and can easily visualize their design.

In your mind's eye, spatial systems allow you to identify significant pictures with specific locations or imagine them positioned along familiar paths. When you need to remember anything, you may travel back in your mind and "discover" the pictures you left behind, which can help you recall key facts quickly and precisely.

Start trying with some of these mnemonic techniques, and you'll rapidly notice that your memory will improve dramatically!

Memory tools – For ages, "mnemonics" have been employed to increase confidence and resist information overload.

Rich imagery, powerful emotions, and obvious patterns are used in the finest memory approaches.

Various particular systems have been developed based on the core ideas of imagination, association, and location.

## AROUND THE WORLD

Memory competitions are held in a variety of ways in different nations.

They may utilize various regulations and provide different

awards, for example. But these are competitions where mind athletes of all stripes fight against one another to showcase their cognitive dominance.

Now:

While no single country's memory athlete tactics are unique, mnemonists from all around the world have perfected old mnemonic techniques to create memory training activities for experts and amateurs alike.

Are you ready to investigate? Let's get started!

## China: Ming Mnemonics To Memorize Classical Poetry Reams

An Italian Jesuit priest became the first westerner to pass China's top civil service tests in the 16th century.

What is the significance of this?

The exam required memorization of reams of ancient poetry, a challenge that only 1% of those who attempted it could do effectively.

Despite never having spoken Chinese before, Ricci passed these tests after just ten years.

How did he pull that off?

Ricci used the Memory Palace approach to do this.

But don't stop there; here's something else to think about:

"Ricci taught the Chinese how to create a Memory Palace," argues Jonathan D. Spence in The Memory Palace of Matteo Ricci.

## WHY IS THE MEMORY PALACE SUPERIOR TO ROTE LEARNING?

The Chinese had their dedicated study techniques, including repetition and recitation as memory aids. This was used with traditional Chinese memory techniques such as mnemonic poetry and rhyming jingles.

In his Treatise on Mnemonic Arts, Ricci stated, "To everything that we intend to remember, we should give an image; and to each of these pictures, we should assign a location where it might slumber calmly until we are ready to recover it by an act of memory."

Ricci proposed three sites for these "mental" structures: they may be based on existing structures, fictitious locales, or a combination of both.

Ricci's memory techniques aid in the memorization of whole books and enormous amounts of terminology.

Plus, there's more.

He also devised a method for remembering Chinese writing.

Memory champions on China's popular reality and talent program, The Brain, have memorized decks of cards or information about airline tickets using Memory Palaces (likely improved versions of Ricci's technique).

Seven players must overcome mental feats such as memorizing the names and birthdays of over 900 newborns or completing a sequence of Rubik's Cube puzzles entirely blindfolded in under five minutes in each episode.

## HOW TO MEMORIZE A DECK OF CARDS CHINESE STYLE – FAST!

Do you want to discover how Chinese mnemonist Wang Feng memorizes a deck of cards?

Feng, a two-time World Memory Champion, used a strategy similar to Ricci's to take use of the brain's innate propensity to remember images and places.

To remember the order of a deck of cards, Feng assigns a two-digit number to each card. He then converts that number into a picture, which he saves in a convenient area from which he can readily retrieve it when needed.

Isn't there a resemblance to Ricci's Memory Palace system?

Now that you know what Ricci's approach is, you may use it to create your own memory training program (like making a gym in your own mind for mental fitness). You may also use the Magnetic Memory Method to make Memory Palaces.

In the end, I feel the Magnetic Memory Method is the preferable option for most students.

What is the reason behind this? Because it not only assists you in remembering the knowledge more quickly, but it also assists you in achieving predictable and dependable permanence that improves with practice.

## MONGOLIA: THE GENGHIS KHAN WAY TO BRAIN STRENGTH

Genghis Khan, the founder of the Mongol Empire, would certainly be delighted to learn that 10 of the top 50 persons in recent global memory rankings are his ancestors!

Mongolia, home to one of the world's last nomadic tribes, aspires to be a titan in the esoteric field of mental sports and utilizes the sport as a means of nation-building.

The Periodic Table of Elements and other cognitive feats are taught at the Mongolian Intellectual Academy utilizing the same principles that control the Memory Palace approach — associating unknown words and numbers to familiar mental images or stories that may be entrenched in a person's long-term memory.

The teacher progresses through the first column of the periodic table, converting letters and numbers into vibrant and absurd visuals. The graphics are backed by a captivating tale that helps students recall the element's name, atomic number, and atomic mass.

There are almost no errors when asked to recollect the period table remembered using this mnemonic approach!

Despite their remarkable accuracy, the Mongolian squad faced stiff competition in the 2015 Extreme Memory Tournament.

*The Opposite were:*

Simon Reinhard, the world's fastest card memorizer and reigning XMT Champion, and Alex Mullen, the 2015 World Memory Champion, were the competitors.

Despite the tough competition, Enhkjin Tumur, a 17-year-old first-time participant, achieved a tournament record by recalling 30 pictures in 14.4 seconds, setting a tournament record.


## CANADA: A HUNTER-GATHERER MEMORY TECHNIQUE

Dave Farrow, a two-time Guinness World Record holder for memorizing 59 decks of cards in order, is a Canadian who has either devised or enhanced memory training techniques for remembering and recalling information with ease.

Farrow employs the Peg System, in which you memorize a series of facts by attaching or pegging them to words or numbers you already know.

Information is literally hung on a number.

## THIS IS WHAT FARROW SAYS ABOUT HIS MEMORY TECHNIQUE:

"Memory techniques work by taking advantage of a natural mechanism in the brain that we all have that allows us to memorize information without any repetition. It's a hunter-gatherer fight or flight mechanism—if you needed repetition to remember where you saw that predator, you would not be alive anymore. What I do, and what I teach people how to do, is manipulate the brain to activate that process at will."

## HOW TO USE COLORS TO REMEMBER NUMBERS?

The Alpha Numeric Spectrum scheme is another way I've heard Farrow mention. This method employs numerical and phonetic codes to help people learn and remember numbers quickly. It utilizes the following arrangement (you can make your own version):

- 1 = red
- 2 = orange
- 3 = yellow
- 4 = green
- 5 = blue
- 6 = purple
- 7 = brown
- 8 = silver
- 9 = gold
- 0 = black

# IMPROVE YOUR MEMORY SPEAKING YOUR MIND'S LANGUAGE

By learning the language your mind uses, you'll be able to tap into your mind's full potential and develop a remarkable memory. It's easier than you think – and you'll actually have fun doing it.

## Your Mind Thinks in Pictures

The brain has evolved to be incredibly efficient at processing sensory information. The mind analyzes the world and makes judgments by accurately interpreting the five senses.

Sight has evolved into the most complex and developed of all the human senses. As a result, human brains have evolved to be extraordinarily adept at retaining and analyzing pictures, particularly those of tangible, real-world things. Attempting to remember abstract symbols, such as words displayed on a page, is wasteful and unnatural. Words are valuable communication units that we have invented, but they are not ideal for our brains to comprehend information.

The true language of the mind is imagery. Images are the

building pieces of your mind's language, serving as its lexicon.

What comes to mind when I ask you to imagine a horse? Is it the letters H-O-R-S-E spelled backwards? Of course not: it's a horse drawing, and you can even tell me what color it is. Isn't it true that dreams are always represented by images? We should take advantage of the fact that pictures are how your mind interacts with us.

## Visual Thinking and Memory

The true language of the brain is imagery. The building blocks of your mind's language are images.

What comes to mind when you're asked to imagine a horse? Is it a combination of the letters H-O-R-S-E? No way: it's a horse drawing, and you can even tell me what color it is. Isn't it true that all dreams are visual? We should take advantage of the fact that pictures are how our minds communicate with us.

- Bacon
- Eggs
- Wine
- Batteries
- Bubble gum
- Milk
- Envelopes
- Spinach
- Coffee
- Tomato

To get started, we'll need some basic vocabulary, just like when learning a new language. Let's start with some extremely useful words: the numbers one through ten. We'll be able to memorize our grocery list or any other list we come across by incorporating numbers into our visual language.

A number can be converted to a picture in a variety of ways. One of my favorites is to utilize photos that resemble the form of the numerals. We'll have far better mental pictures to play with if we get rid of abstract symbols and replace them with lively, dynamic, and colorful images.

*Here are a few recommendations:*

- Candle
- Swan
- Heart
- Sailboat
- Hook
- Golf club
- Cliff
- Snowman
- Balloon with string
- Dinner plate and fork

To help you visualize the similarities, here's a graphical representation of the list:

Feel free to experiment with different photos to see what works best for you. Please take your time to familiarize yourself with your list once you've completed it. These will be our pegs, and after you've learnt them, you'll be able to utilize them to memorize just about anything you desire.

### Connecting Images

We can memorize new pictures by creating associations between them now that we've built a basic lexicon of pictures. All we have to do now is mix the two photos to create a new one. Now is the moment to let your imagination run wild since your new image must meet just one requirement: it must be completely ridiculous!

After all, these are the things that are remembered, aren't they? Make it wacky, stupid, obnoxious, odd, amazing, animated, senseless. Make the situation so one-of-a-kind that it could never occur in real life. The only rule is that if something is uninteresting, it is incorrect.

Let's return to our previous example of a grocery list. What is the relationship between the number 1 (candle) and our first shopping item (bacon)?

To begin, imagine a very large and powerful candle being used for frying bacon at a fast-food restaurant. Make an effort to enhance the image in your mind: concentrate on the bacon strips for a moment or two, making them as vivid as possible. Even better if you use your other senses: smell the bacon and hear it being fried. Add some movement and craziness: couldn't the bacon strips be screaming for help in the frying pan? Did I mention that it should be zany?

Let's try it again, this time linking the numbers "2" (swan) and "egg."

It won't work if a swan lays an egg since it's too evident. Consider the mother swan depositing the egg in the same manner as a woman giving birth: in a surgical room, surrounded by other swans disguised as physicians. Put the father swan in the room and proudly videotape everything. Finally, everyone is taken aback - it's three eggs: triplets!!

Isn't it ridiculous? There's no doubt about that. Is it effective? Yes, absolutely.

You've probably figured it out by now. It may seem like doing this for each item is a lot of effort at first, but it isn't. This mental game becomes natural – and enjoyable!

There's not much more to do when it's time to recall the list: the recalling procedure is automated. The following is a rough outline of how it works: You think to yourself, 'What's the first item?' and the picture of a candle flashes over your thoughts. Sure enough, leaping bacon slices appear a fraction of a second later!

## HOW DOES IT COMPARE TO TRADITIONAL MEMORIZATION?

It's time to see how you fared on our memory test. Try to write down all of the items in sequence without consulting the original list. Give yourself a point for each accurate word, plus an extra point if the word is in the proper place.

How did you fare in the competition? The majority of people get a 12 out of a potential 20 on average. When you ask them again a week later (without informing them), the average drops to a dismal 5.

The findings are astounding when using the pegging method: the average score is a perfect 20 – even when participants are polled a week later. That's simply after the first time I used the procedure.

The pegging memorizing method is only one example of how effective visual thinking can be. In reality, visual thinking is at the heart of many mind-enhancement techniques like mind mapping and most other sophisticated memorizing techniques.

# MEMORY TRAINING

Mnemonics are basic memory aids that allow you to relate common, quickly remembered things and concepts to the information you wish to remember. You can afterward recollect what you wanted to remember by memorizing these commonplace facts.

The Number/Rhyme Technique — This technique aids in the recall of ordered lists. Begin with a common phrase that rhymes with the number (we suggest 1 – Bun, 2 – Shoe, 3 – Tree, 4 – Door, 5 – Hive, 6 – Bricks, 7 – Heaven, 8 – Gate, 9 – Line, and 10 – Hen). Then make an image that connects each to the item you're attempting to recall. Start with: to recall a list of South American nations using number/rhyme:

- One – Bun/Colombia: A BUN with the column of a Greek temple coming out of it.
- Two – Shoe/Venezuela: Venus de Milo coming out of the sea on a SHOE.
- Three – Tree/Guyana: Friends call GUY and Anna sitting in a TREE.
- Four – Door/Ecuador: A DOOR in the shape of a circle/globe with a golden Equator|running around it.

Create images that relate to the shape of each number, then tie those pictures to the items on your list using the Number/Shape System. Let's continue with the same example:

- One – Spear/Columbia: The shaft of the SPEAR is a thin marble COLUMn.
- Two – Swan/Venezuela: This time, Venus is standing on the back of a SWAN.
- Three – Bifocal Glasses/Guyana: GUY has just trodden on Anna's bifocals. She's quite cross!
- Four – Sailboat/Ecuador: The boat is sailing across the golden line of the Equator on a globe.

The Alphabet Technique — For lists of more than 9 or 10 items, this method works effectively (beyond 10, the previous techniques can get too difficult). Instead of looking for a term that rhymes with the number, you use this technique to identify the items you wish to remember with a letter of the alphabet, from A to Z. This is a quick way to recall a list of up to 26 things in sequence.

The Traveling System – Consider a familiar route or excursion in your thoughts, such as going from your office to your house. Each landmark on your journey should be associated with the things you wish to remember. You can recall a lot of things if your journey is long enough and well-known!

The Roman Room System - This procedure employs locations to boost your memory. The Roman Room System. Connect to a familiar room or location of your list of objects. In your kitchen, at your workplace, or in a familiar food shop, you may find associations with objects.

## CHALLENGE YOUR BRAIN

Your mind requires exercise, as with other aspects of your body. You may practice your brain regularly by utilizing it in various ways. Try this: Try

- **Learn a new skill or start a hobby** – Find activities to strengthen abilities you usually do not utilize in your everyday life. For example, you cultivate your creative side with painting lessons or photography if you deal with mathematics throughout the day.
- **Use visualization on a regular basis** – Since many memories include the combination and reminder of visuals, strengthening this skill is vital. Get a lot of work with this!

- **Keep active socially** – You must be vigilant when communicating and interacting with others. This helps to keep your brain active and robust.

- **Focus on the essential things** – You may not recall it all, so be sure that you offer important things to accomplish to your brain - and don't overburden it by "trash." The principle of "waste in, waste out."

*Tip:*

Although developing a good memory is crucial, remembering anything superfluous (like jobs or stuff to purchase) is hard. It is also crucial to accomplish things. Moreover, they might lessen your capacity to concentrate on other things since they drain short-term memory. You might also be agitated as you strive to keep all the things you need to do in mind.

Write down this stuff in your list of to-do! You mustn't recall it all in that manner. And you know how to seek for the knowledge you need if your memory fails.

Stay active in your brain using memory games and puzzles – Try Sudoku, chess, Scrabble, Word Twist and trivia games, matching pairs, puzzles, and much more. These are great strategies to memorize while enjoying. And investigate areas such as Lumosity for brain training as a method to enhance your thinking.

Your memory is a precious thing to keep and improve. The capacity to record knowledge fast and properly is still crucial even if you no longer have to memorize knowledge for examinations.

You must rely on your memory, whether you remember the name of someone you met at a conference last month or you remember the turnover of the past quarter. Learn to maintain your mind healthy and practice the ideas above.

You just have one brain — treat it well, practice it a lot, and don't take it for granted. You never know if you will have to be in good shape!

# MEMORY TRICKS TO HELP YOU REMEMBER ANYTHING EASILY

It is easy to reject a remarkable memory as a useless ability in the era of Google and Wikipedia. You won't have internet access occasionally, however. Sometimes reading aloud might give you an awful impression, such at an interview or when you deliver a speech.

So, a good memory can be a great benefit until your talk is coded into a chip in your brain. Simple story strategies to boost your memory are provided here:

### 1. Clench Your Right Hand When Learning, Then Your Left Hand to Remember

Just as strange as it may appear, this has really been shown to improve short-term memory. Research. Just tighten your right hand in the fist when you learn. And then pinch your left hand afterward if you need to recall.

However, this has been demonstrated exclusively with rectangular people. Although they ran the same test for leftists, the findings are for another research, so keep tuned. These results will not change.

Or just test yourself and see if you have any substantial changes.

### 2. Coordinate Smells

Smells have been demonstrated to evoke more memories than sound, however it might be fairly tricky for any practical application of this information.

One suggestion is to synchronize the fragrances when you memorize anything to remember. For example, when you read the perfume, try spraying it with a very distinct smell on the back of your hand and then the same day on your test, talk or presentation again.

### 3. Coordinate Positions

It is probably simpler to access your memories when you keep the same posture you tried to recall as you did when you memorized. Thus, while the study focused on autobiographical recollections, additional practical circumstances should be included.

Try to study in one posture – e.g. with your legs crossed at a specific angle – and then remember to answer the test.

### 4. Chew Gum

Two ideas exist that explain why this is. Firstly, chewing leads to increased blood flow in the region and increases the brain's activity. The other is the same as our previous tricks: chewing gum is linked with memory. So if you chew gum while remembering it, it becomes simpler to access.

No matter what you think, picking a pack of rubber before your next big test could be a smart idea. And if the taste has the same impact as that of scent, stick to the exam with the same taste as when you study.

### 5. Use the Power of Melody

The easiest way to recall lyrics is to recite words of a tuneless essay. It is nearly strange. And we don't just imagine that either. The effectiveness of music in learning has been demonstrated through studies.

You may just piggyback songs that you already know and enjoy, even if it may seem like tons of labor. Maybe the finest are famous classics because they have no lyrics, which might distract you when you try to learn.

Just be sure that when you recall, you don't break into song!

### 6. Don't Do "All-Nighters"

In addition to improving sleep, a repeat of your memory is recommended not just in order to reduce your memory even immediately.

It is also demonstrated to function better than mass practice, i.e. clutching, when distributed practice is being studied over lengthy periods. Don't do every night. Don't do every night.

After a day of study, remember to get your sleep hours.

And it's obviously a terrific idea to study anything a few minutes a day, a bit at a time. When you study a language, it's quite handy to use flashcards or decent language learning tools.

### 7. Meditate

As it turns out, Buddhists have been on to something in the belief that meditation is a path to enlightenment. In a study, meditating four times per day for 20 minutes increased cognition from 15 percent to as much as 50 percent.

So start practicing it if you've ever thought about meditation. See the fast and simple meditation guide: a 5-minute meditation guide: Anywhere, Anytime.

### 8. Exercise More

If you're tedious about any other recommendations and want a physical approach, you're lucky. A clear link between regular exercise and better cognitive functioning, including memory, has been shown. This would make you not only healthier but also better your memory. Exercise more.

If you believe you're too busy to practice.

## 9. Drink Less

Long-term alcohol addiction has shown serious memory impairments. And though I'm not accusing you of being an alcoholic, I believe many of us can take a bit less to drink.

I am very sure we can all agree that excessive drinking is not the best way to memorize anything when adding in the time you lose when drinking.

## 10. Associate

Tricks that enhance memory are all based on one thing: association.

Up to now, we have largely dealt with unintentional associations such as better remembering or sitting in the same position while smelling the same odor. However, this is the moment for a voluntary partnership.

It's rather straightforward in specific areas:

One strategy in linguistic learning, for example, is to link the new word with a term you already know that sounds. You know what I am talking about if you have observed how much easier it is to remember a new term that sounds precisely like the other.

Sometimes, like the Japanese term kensaku, you must extend the pronunciation a bit, which I recall from 'Ken sucks.' The more distant and ludicrous the organization in my personal experience, the simpler it is to recall. (Kensaku ostensibly means search.)

And then visual connection with new words has been much simpler with many new textbooks that aid to adopt visual strategies, particularly the chinese alphabet with "Heisig" approach being reasonably well recognized and liked in communities of language learning.

The Heisig approach involves visual association to remind Chinese people of the form of hanzi or kanji. It was regarded as highly useful by some of my friends and was mediocre by others.

## 11. Bundle Memories Together

Make use and combine a lot of memories into one pattern recognition.

Perhaps the easiest element is to recall numbers. The 'chunking technique' is named this. It can make it much simpler to recall sequences of numbers if you can bind them together meaningfully, which signifies something to you."

We bundle telephone number numbers in pairs in Norway so that you may think about them for years, for example. (There are 8 digits in our telephone numbers.) Therefore, there may be a 45 80 90 18 phone number. Thus it was possible to choose 1945 when WWII was over and 80 were associated with the 1980s and 90 with the 1990s.

## 12. Write It Out

Perhaps it's the extra repetition or perhaps the fact that writing triggers entirely different brain sections and thus stores knowledge in more than one location.

So, if anything you don't forget is essential, write it out by hand. Better still, create a real note and bring it to yourself.

This way, you remember more often, even when your mobile phone has malfunctioned, or the sound is mistakenly turned off.

## 13. Talk to Yourself

As the solitary spectator, you don't have to do theatrical

monologs in the long run. Just say whatever you want loudly to remember. Research has shown that memory accuracy has increased by up to 10%. So perhaps it's a better-exercised habit in loneliness.

*Bottom Line*

Although some of them are gimmicks, others will grow and improve your cognitive skills generally. Of course, the later will complement the former so remember, if you want to increase your memory, take charge of yourself and your brain.

As for the techniques themselves, several tricks can produce the best outcome, as the greatest method to recreate something is by replicating a whole environment.

# LEARN HOW TO MEMORIZE SEQUENCES OF PLAYING CARDS

Have you ever read the World Memory Championships or been watching?

The memory of the sequencing of a map is one of the events. So you have to look through the deck (the memory phase) and then talk to an adjudicator about the order (the recall phase).

In less than 15 seconds, the quickest competitors can save a pack!!! (This introduction probably takes roughly the duration).

How long do you believe it takes you to store a pack?

Well, unless you're a memory athlete, or you're a scientist, or you could be struggling to recall the sequence of more than 10 cards or even an entire bucket in less than 15 seconds. Instead, I think that's what we are talking about.

ATTENTION! I will not lie to you. You'll be disappointed if you're searching for a 5-minute magic approach to achieve this! No such technique exists. It takes great time and effort on your behalf to learn this method.

But if you want to find out a strategy that allows you to store a card deck in five minutes, then you will read on. Before your training begins, think of yourself as a Rocky or Karate Kid.

Maybe you would like to create a baseline for comparative reasons before you start. For example, see how many cards you can recall right now and how long you need to save that amount.

## THE DIFFICULTY WITH RECALLING PLAYING CARDS

It takes a minute to analyze why it is so hard to memorize a card deck before we enter the memorization procedure.

They're boring! They're boring! Tedious, boring, boring, boring, boring. They're 52 really identical pieces of card. Our memory favors intriguing stuff.

You're accused. There is no actual appearance pattern (unless you take the time to order them by suit and rank). We prefer our memories of known patterns.

## The solution

There are two difficulties, as we have observed, with the memory of a card deck:

- The cards themselves are not clear enough to function with our memory.
- A pattern has to be created to assist keep us in mind card order.

Fortunately, two well-established memory methods may be used to resolve these issues.

- The system Person/Object to make the cards memorable.
- The sequence recall system of the Roman Room.

## The Person / Object system

We will assign a person and an object to every playing card in the deck. The reason is that remembering the person or item is much simpler than an abstract card suit and value.

We will also recall pairs of our cards. For this purpose, we take the person in the pair for the first card and the item in the pair for the second. Then we put them together in action.

Various memory specialists employ different versions on this topic. The one that we will employ is the Dominic System - a world champion Dominic O'Brien's system.

## The basis of the system

The technique is based on changing numbers to letters. We look at card numbers 1 (Ace) through 10 for our needs. (We're going to look separately at courtroom cards). In the system, the letters are assigned to the following numbers:

| | |
|---|---|
| 1 = A | 6 = S |
| 2 = B | 7 = G |
| 3 = C | 8 = H |
| 4 = D | 9 = N |
| 5 = E | 10 = O |

These are then combined with the correspondence letters:

| | |
|---|---|
| Clubs = C | Hearts = H |
| Diamonds = D | Spades = S |

For the Nine Spades, the initials would therefore be NS (9=N and Spades=S).

We may proceed with the same premise for court cards (Jacks, Queens and Kings)—the Jack of Clubs initials are made to JC. Otherwise, other relationships might be established. All Jacks, for example, maybe renowned persons named Jack.


## FACTORS THAT INFLUENCE OUR MEMORY

Some of the factors that serve to consolidate our memory of specific things may be valuable at this point.

- **Our senses.** Can you remember the scent of a coffee jar newly opened? Or a broken garlic bulb? Honey flavor or citrus juices? A favorite music or song? A cat's fur feeling, or the discomfort of hemming your toe on the leg of the table?
- **Humour.** Funny stuff is unforgettable. Regardless if Basil Fawlty is giving his malfunctioning automobile 'a pretty good beating' in The Big Bang Theory, humor tends to be remembered. Whether it is Sheldon's lack of social skills.
- **Exaggeration.** Don't just photograph something in its regular size — imagine it merely minute or enormous.

- **Order.** Our brains want things that can make sense of, not something entirely random, in an orderly pattern.

- **Bright and colourful.** Rainbows are more attractive than rainwaters.

- **Sex.** They say 'sex sells,' and it surely builds an image for our minds when it comes to our memories.

- **Imagination.** In the process that we undertake, this will play a big role. You will be the biggest asset in your imagination.

## An Illustration Of The System

Now, at the time this is all a bit abstract, so let's have a few instances to show how this works. The Ace of Spades and the Three of Diamonds are the two cards we want to remember.

For the Ace Spades, A and S are the letters, while for the Three

Spades, the letters C and D are the letters.

So, now we have to select a remembered person and a connected object for each of those initials.

It's often easier to find renowned people: TV and movie stars, sports stars, comedians, songwriters, explorers, caricatures and others. In addition, you can employ friends and relatives.

Choose folks who you can quickly see - the much better if you actually love or loathe them.

Take some minutes to choose your person with the AS and CD initials before I give you my options. Then, after you read my selections, I suggest this because it could be harder for anybody else to conceive of, as my decisions will continue to appear in your thoughts.

Done it?

Alright, my choices were:

AS = Arnold Schwarzenegger (object – sunglasses used in the Terminator films)

CD = Cameron Diaz (object – sequin dress, as worn in the Mask dance scene)

Now we would have Arnie on the first pair with the order of

two cards and the second pair with the sequin outfit. Then we put the two together in motion.

Okay, we will mix Arnie's picture with sequin clothing! We will utilize our creativity, exaggeration and humor.


Arnie is a large person, particularly in his Mr. Olympia days, if we think of him. The sequin dress of Cameron Diaz would have been rather tiny. Picture a gigantic Arnie crammed into a bit of sequin dress. Massively muscled! What a sight!

Imagine him now dancing, like John Travolta, blazing dazzling lights on a sequin outfit and "Staying alive" hammering from some big voices.

And you got it there. The Ace of the Spades and The Three of the Diamonds are unforgettable images.

## BUILDING YOUR OWN PACK OF CARDS

Okay, this is the hardest portion of the entire system, perhaps.

You must now think of individuals and stuff to match all 52 cards.

Create a grid of 1 to 10 digits including Jack, Queen, and King, and suit Clubs, Diamonds, Hearts, and Spades to top it all. Note the combinations of letters for items 1 to 10.

Some of these are quite easy for you. Others could take some time.

The ones who come to you effortlessly are usually the ones with which you can work comfortably. Those you have to work with can do a bit more.

Once you have reached the stick, be sure not to brainstorm yourself with your family, friends or Google.

What you can choose is without any restrictions. True or fictitious. Good or bad. Good or terrible, awful. Dead or living. - Dead or living. Anything that works for you.

### The Roman Room system

There are several names in this system. You may hear it being:

- The Roman Room system
- The Method of Loci
- The Journey System
- The Memory Palace

The method works by integrating the information to be saved with information about an existing well known environment.

The famous environment is often a recognized travel or construction and has been constructed in ancient Roman times (hence the various names used above).

You will remember that our brains are like order from the factors that impact our memory (like!). This is the system of the Roman Room.

You may also recall the renowned champion of the memorial palace, the legendary investigator Sherlock Holmes.

Picture your rooms at home. The more data you have, the better your location, size, look, function, and objects within them.

As we recall the cards in pairs and 52 cards in the deck, 26 distinct places need to be created.

Now we need to be a bit créative unless you are fortunate

enough to own a house with so many rooms!

Include those if you have a garden or gardens. A garage for your automobile, an outdoor parking garage, courtyard spaces, toilets, closets, staircase, steps, luggage compartments, bathrooms and a loft.

It will help to write the places in a list from 1 to 26 if you have a piece of paper. You might have to jig a few times to reach the last list.

Now select a place of departure and picture the journey between the different sites. The path you would follow in real life must be a sensible one, not suddenly disappearing into one spot and reappearing into another which is not related!. It should be a sensible one.

Have a voyage repeated till it becomes second nature (in your head, don't run like a madman about your house!). The travel sequence is crucial since that is what will add to the memory of your cards the "order" sequence.

A quick re-cap

Let's remember what we covered up to now.

- It is tough to memorize playing cards (let alone remembering a whole deck in order).
- Memory strategies are available that we may employ to alleviate this problem.
- The Dominic System enables us to recognize the player cards (do you recall the pictures for the Spades As and the Diamonds Three?).
- Knowing which aspects affect memory allows us to generate lively pictures.
- The method of the Roman Room helps us remember cards.

All right, so now it is time to make excellent use of what we learned.

## Let's memorise some cards!

You have therefore made your card deck of Dominic System and your voyage in the Roman Room. You're ready! You're ready!

Well, almost ready. Almost. At this point, I should add a little caution.

For many individuals, like me, the technique is so effective that you can hardly forget a specific sequence of cards when the initial start is done so that you can memorize the following series.

So, don't try running before you can walk. Instead, I recommend you restrict yourself to one sequence a day.

Take your card deck and make it a great shuffle—this is time to save your imagination on the deck of cards.

### The approach

- Slowly, go through the deck two cards at a time.
- Recall your association for the first card (the person).
- And the second card (the object).
- Recall the first location for your Roman Rooms journey.
- Now, remembering the memory influencing factors that we considered earlier, combine the card pair with the location.

- Make sure that the image is vivid and clear.

- Move on to the next pair and next location. Form the next image.

- Keep going until you have gone through the pack.

- Give yourself a few seconds and then begin to run through the journey in your mind, visualizing the created card pair images at each location.

- If there are any holes in your recall you can have another run through if you like. Really focus on those person/object/location combinations.

- Time to test yourself!!!

- Hold the deck in your hands and say out loud the name of the playing card before turning it over. Then the next, and the next and so on.

- If you get stuck move on (it is likely that you will have to skip 2 cards as we are memorizing in pairs) until you reach the end of the deck.

## How many did you get?

**52**

Well done. You've clearly got an excellent grasp of the techniques involved.

**40 to 50**

Pretty good. You have a good grasp of the techniques but just need more practice.

**Less than 40**

OK, something needs a little more work. Where did you struggle?

## Strengthening of associations – cards

You need to do additional work here before you try to memorize any further decks if you cannot remember the cards' person/object details.

You may record your associations on your cell phone and play them on your way to and from work or any travel you may take.

A card (or card) can be chosen from the day. Think of the card of the day all day long when you have free time. For example, you wake up in the bathroom. Having breakfast. Getting dressed. Going to work. Having lunch. Taking a walk. Having coffee.

Another method you may use is what I call the approach 'I have your number!' Whenever you look at a combination of numbers, you think about your Dominic System cards.

Have you seen No. 16 on a bus front? What does it mean? Come on, that's what you know – The first is A, the six is S. The Spades Ace. Who and what are the objects of the person?

You may use it with numbers on pretty much anything; home numbers, auto registration numbers, telephone numbers, the next time you pay something.

Likewise, if you encounter a person or item group, attempt to remember the card in question. For example, Cameron Diaz just saw on TV - which card do you think about?

## Strengthening the associations – the locations
Have you had difficulty remembering the room sequence?

If so, you just have to imprint the travel into your memory in the time you dedicate. Are you struggling with one particular location? Try to make the connection to the prior location more remembered.

Let's just suppose that your kitchen is at the end of your hardwood hallway. The kitchen in the sequence is missing.

Think of an excessively sloping hardwood floor. Not only a bit

— this floor is so slick that you fight to stay upright, even with very strong trainers. When you're in the corridor, your feet slide continually out from underneath the cartoon characters, arms twisting around while they are trying to stay in balance.

Now, let's assume the cooker portrays one of the biggest pieces of equipments in the kitchen. The door continues opening and closing as if it is some kind of monstrous mouth attempting to consume you. This cooker is gigantic and is alive. And HEAT! It is amazing, the cooker has dragon-like features and every time the door/mouth swings open breathes flames.

So, when you enter the hallway, what happens? You're gliding and sliding. Everything you do to try to stop has nothing to do with it. Instead, you are sneaking unchecked into the kitchen ... and the cooker of the Devil is trying to incinerate you!

There is now an integrally connected hall and kitchen. I don't think you will forget the link again, rather improbable.

### Strengthening the associations – the combinations

It's the mixture of both you are fighting to learn the Dominic method and the Roman Rooms method and still fight.

I sympathise. I struggled with this for a while too.

Our creativity is, honestly, AWESOME when we are children. We have no difficulty with the most unbelievable stuff. But we tend to utilize less of our imagination as we become older. And it might be a question of 'use or lose' as with many things!

The good news is that you will soon get back to the swing of things when you begin to use it again. Can you remember the two places we connected in the preceding section?

Floor slippery? Hell's cooker? All is the hall and the cuisine. This is it.

Well, it's basically about the same method, except the cards are included.

I don't want to spoil any card associations you can build like before, so I'm going to stick to the examples we have already used. So we're going to change the cards so it's Diamonds Three first, then Spades Ace afterward. And the kitchen is the place we desire.

Do you recall the Three of Diamonds person and the Ace of Spade's object?

This is Cameron Diaz and the sunglasses of Terminator.

So, let's start building that image.

In the kitchen, picture Cameron. What are her clothes? Is her clothing wearing?! What's her hairstyle? Is it regular size, or is it miniaturized? Does she wear perfume, or does she smell like Eau de Dog Poo, which is appealing? Is she frightened (thinks where she is ... with the Hell stove!) or is she confident?

Sunlasses picture. Does Cameron wear them as usual (maybe to shield her against the cooker's fire)? Is it because she is at home, or are they flipped on her head? Or her top tucked? Do you have any kind of extraordinary capabilities that guarantee cooker protection?

Kitchen photo. We know the cooker is burning from Hell. We know it. How is Cameron connected to it and the sunglasses?

Putting everything together...

The cooker of the kitchen is as stupid as ever. An explosion of flames explodes from it every time the door opens. The guest is outraged.

Cameron is in a bikini and has a sunscreen factor of 6000! His heat is not bothering in the kitchen at all. She takes a drink with one hand (a Snowball, just to add to the Hell combination). On the contrary, she holds...

The lenses of sunlight. However, she hold the darkened lenses with her arms held to the cooker for the fire because ... every arm has saucers and the cooker grills them with the fire!

Naturally, all bullshit. This is the point, however. However.

Every day is uninteresting and immediately forgotten, openly and daily. We desire an uncommon item. Strange. Funny. Funny. Funny. Scary. Blissful. Sexy. (Were the Spice Girls' original names?)

### Improving your time

You will be certain that once you reach the level when you can store a card deck every time you try, you will have the time to go to the last step - clockwise memorizations.

Begin to note how long a deck of cards will take to memorize. When you collect the deck, the time begins and finishes when you reinstate it. The actual callback section of the job is not included.

With your watch, cell phone or Excel and some VBA, you can timeline yourself.

Initially, aim to get under 15 minutes. Then 10 minutes. Then 5 minutes.

My best time is 3 minutes 52 seconds.

At the time of writing the World Record time is 12.74 seconds!

# MEMORY ENHANCEMENT

The improvement of memory is vital in three areas: productivity, personal growth and prevention. So regardless of whether you are expanding your business or your employment, alignment or standing ahead of potential health issues, this article might make or destroy your efforts through easy memory boosting tactics.

If you look a bit at enhancing memory, you will discover that you may concentrate on several categories.

Three categories will be looked upon – nutrition (what we put into the body), physical (what we are doing with the body) and mental (tools and hacks we can use to train our brains).

For many, what we put in front of us goes uncontrolled. It's normally a weight loss, but most nutritional factors affect our brain, which affects our remember. When we filter what we eat or drink.

Your intellect is an enormous asset at work. Your productivity will affect whether you are sharp or mentally fluid. Enhancing memory provides you a smoother course while dealing with huge business initiatives.

# 1. WATER

Nutritionally, water is the first component to boost memory. Drinking more water is so prevalent that they offer applications to track your consumption of water.

Many admonish themselves, in a broad sense, since it is good for you since they should drink more water, but there are special advantages to drinking more water when improving memory.

While the body consists of 60% water, the brain consists of 73% water. In addition, the American Journals of Clinical Nutrition showed that "the memory and focused attention increased with consuming water."

For me, from the water bottle, I drink more water. My water consumption falls by more than half without my water bottle. Once you find the approach to drink the most water, bring the procedure to bed and bed all day long so that the following morning it is ready for you first.

# 2. FATS

Like water, a substantial part of our brain is made up of lipids.

Fats nourish our brain to the optimal degree of slow-burning energy. To increase memory, it makes a difference in your diet to find the right combination of beneficial fats combined with fruits and vegetables.

A Harvard Health publication report indicated "polyunsaturated fats might be the food combat heroes for the preservation of memory." The nuts, olive oil and salmon may contain these fats.

You do not have to gulp a gallon of fish oil to receive omega 3 fatty acids everyday. You may begin by simply arranging what you consume and observing your mental clarity. For example, add a few eggs rather than carbohydrates for breakfast. Replace the snack with a handful of almonds instead of a refined sugar snack in the afternoon.

You don't have to reach the extremes; simply start playing with your food sequence all day long and find out where your mind benefits most from extra fats.

## 3. SUPPLEMENTS

You may also improve your memory using nutrients, including pills for fish oil. Unfortunately, the market of supplements is vast and many promises are not based on clinical studies on increased cognitive functions.

If you find supplements to improve your memory, the easiest way to do this is to look for your selections. If you want supplements with measured, impartial findings, look for blind and double blind research.

Like any of these strategies, always look for and test what works best for you.

## 4. INTERMITTENT FASTING

Intermittent fasting has been on the rise in recent years. Intermittent fasting, common in the domain of weight loss, also has beneficial effects on brain and body chemistry.

There can be numerous ways of intermittent quicking. One of the most typical regimens is to rapidly consume 16 hours of your usual daily calories in an 8-hour diet.

Many reports of intermittent fasting mental clarity and studies indicate why the brain operates in a fasted condition. With the advantage of higher growth hormone and intermittent fasting therapeutic effects, greater mental capability is worthwhile.

# 5. SLEEP

It is quite clear to notice that your memory declines substantially with sleep deprivation. But many of us don't think of sleep as a memory enhancing bridge with our hectic lifestyles.

A Beth Israeli Medical Center research concluded that "the sleep of a good night causes brain modifications, which contribute to better remembrance.

*Here are some useful techniques for improved sleep if you have difficulties getting to sleep:*

- Turn off your devices an hour before bed
- Meditate for 10 minutes prior to sleep
- Eliminate alcohol or caffeine before bed
- Try a natural supplement like Melatonin
- Take up this night routine to get better rest at night

Sleep is a simple way to have the correct operation of your brain and helps to minimize cognitive decay and loss of memory. However, the hardest aspect of your sleep may be to challenge your routines or restrict your idea of keeping you from sleeping.

## 6. EXERCISE

Training is good for the health of the brain. For example, researchers observed that the Hippocampus size, the brain region involved in language memory and learning, appeared to be boosted by regular aerobic exercise.

Exercise might be as easy as a 10 minute stroll or 5 minutes. The point here is that when the body is activated, the mind is activated.

If you do not exercise right now, start small and go up

When you practice a lot, find techniques to increase your memory awareness in your physical workout.

## 7. MASSAGE

Massage is an awareness bridge. Time stays motionless, your body is relaxed, the ability of your brain.

Often, the occupation of life impedes our memory and cognitive performance. Our lists include too many tasks. Our living habits have left little or no room to calm our heads. We have pushed our brains into this impossible atmosphere.

Massage may be an essential pause to the noisy conversation in our thoughts, enabling a brain environment to breathe as our memory improves.

## 8. MEDITATION

Like massage, meditation enables our brain to breathe and relax the hectic dialogue.

One advantage of massage meditation is how fast we reach a more tranquil mind. However, although many people often state they wish to meditate, it is difficult for them to keep their thoughts still and relax in peaceful meditation.

Meditation is just breathing in its simplest form. Special sentences or precise locations are not needed.

Just sit down and take a deep breath for as little as 5 minutes to begin started. There are going to be thoughts coming and going. Just get back to concentrate on your breathing.

With this 5-minute Meditation Guide, you may also try wherever, everytime.

When you do it every day, you will begin to realize how cool you feel in such a short period.

## 9. BATCHING

Batching refers to related jobs in consolidated time-blocks sometimes being utilized to optimize workflow. You might check email once a morning and once an afternoon, for instance, rather than check email throughout the day.

You can see how to reduce the distractions so that your brain focuses on what's in store.

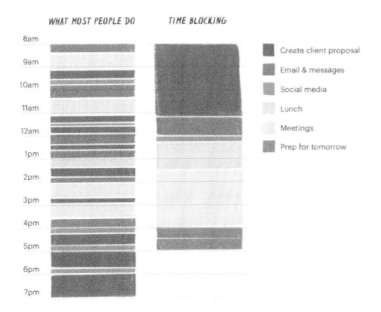

In one study, investigators discovered that the typical brain takes around 20 minutes to refocus following an interruption. Even more importantly, every 11 minutes, a fresh break occurs, which will never entirely catch your brains. This tires and affects your brain's memory.

You simply reduce the number of breaks your brain needs to handle by batching to make it accessible for the tasks that you want to complete.

## 10. GAMES

Brain games can sharply maintain their minds. Memory games

may be entertaining, whether you play on paper or on an app.

Whether games like crossword puzzles truly improve your memory is debated, but the evidence is emerging showing 'brain training' is an effective answer.

Like developing muscles, you urge your brain to develop if you push it beyond its existing capacity. Brain games are a terrific approach to increase your mind when you move your brain to the next level.

## 11. APPS

Apps are fantastic mind trainers, just like games. A vast array of storage and brain workout applications are available.

Here are their top 5 brain training applications among hundreds of brain training applications today:

- Lumosity
- Elevate
- Peak
- Fit Brains
- Cognifit

More brain training applications are also available here to train your mind and increase your memory.

You will want to select one that works best for you at various pricing ranges. In minor waiting intervals in the day, applications may be a terrific answer if you are busy.

## 12. MNEMONIC DEVICES

Fantasy is a strong instrument. In order to easily recall things like names and lists, mnemonic devices employ wordplay.

Mnemonics are popular for: music, rhymes, words/expressions, connection, spelling and images.

*This is an example of a visual mnemonic device for immediate retrieval:*

You will discover a rhyming phrase with each number using numbers 1 to 10 and set that item in your header picture.

You may use it for names, birthdays, job projects or tests: Our example is a food list.

One runs rhymes. So I'm taking a horse track on the track with a horse. Of course, the first thing on my food list is olives, so I can place olives on the horse running saddle to the size of the human being.

It is crucial that the objects in these images are remembered, such as an olive tree in human size on a horse.

For this particular mnemonic technique, common rhyme terms are:

- One, run
- Two, zoo
- Three, tree
- Four, door
- Five, hive

You may start using colors to differentiate groups of 10 if you have 20 items to remember. For instance, if I have 20 food items, the first 10 visualizations can be red and the second one may be yellow in the same rhyming phrases.

Try it and you will see how fast it works. The mind is strong, particularly when we employ pictures that communicate tales. Mnemonic devices are basically hacks that employ graphics and visuals that convey us easy stories.

# HOW TO LEARN (ALMOST) ANYTHING

Have you ever read an educational book, only to recall just a few key elements afterward, if any? The problem may be that you use one of the least effective techniques to learn.

## THE CONE OF LEARNING

When I took music classes at school approximately seven years ago, I recall a wall poster that caught my interest. It was not hard to draw your views to a random item, as our Scottish teacher had nothing in the way of keeping you engaged at the moment. The poster described how we recall things and how different activities boost our chances of remembering anything.

I noticed that the poster material was based on Edgar Dale's work back in 1969, doing some study. Dale examined the most successful learning modes by teaching identical content to people and observed the capacity to retract knowledge after education had been done.

Today, many of you may recognize this as the Learning Cone,

but beware that while the cone is based on the results of the Dale research, Dale never referenced the percentage numbers and added them by others after the first inquiry.

Although the widely used Cone of Learning contains erroneous statistics, it references the most efficient learning processes from which the human brain may obtain information and retain it.

*We can observe this on the basis of the research:*

- Listen to a lecture on the subject or read information about it as the least effective means of learning.
- Teaching others and using them in our own life is the most effective approach to learn something.

The Learning Cone reveals why you recall sections of a movie more probable than you are in a book on the same subject. This is because a movie utilizes aural and visual features, which are more likely to be stored and collected by the brain (memory).

Learning Almost Anything

Once we have thrown out the wrong estimates for a percentage, we must still follow the cone as a guideline, which might fluctuate based on the student's learning style or subject. In addition, various elements such as what you want to remember and how often you use them can dramatically affect your memory. That being said, the cone is another excellent guidance for improved memory imprinting.

In this connection, I considered it a good idea to look at the best ways of using the notion of Cone of Learning and apply it to a practical scenario with which we might relate. So the example I will give in the following recommendations is to look at the best way to understand what yoga is and remember the required poses.

- **Give a Lecture.** Although a lecture is one of the worst methods to recall what you are given, it is one of the most effective to give a lecture. For example, you can go to a university or college and deliver a lecture on the subject of yoga and the various poses.
- **Write an Article.** You can spend time compiling an essay about what yoga is all about and the frequently employed exercises for this meditation if you have a blog or a website. You may also design pictures to

clarify various actions involved, which may be utilized on the site.

- **Make a Video.** Even if you don't have your blog or website, you may publish your movies for free from various video portals such as Youtube and Metacafe. This is successful since you can educate in the framework of a lecture, but we know that you educate a potentially global audience.

- **Discuss with Your Friends.** The individuals of your social circle are one of the easiest teaching possibilities for you. Bring a topic up and offer your rich expertise when appropriate. Wherever possible. The more people you can talk about it in the future, the better it will be for you to recall.

- In addition, it literally may be discussed online in hundreds of ways utilizing online boards, Twitter or even social specialty networks.

- **Do it Yourself.** It doesn't help to try your best to teach others about Yoga if you don't want it and you don't do it yourself. If you teach others the significance of regulating their respiration, you must be sure that you regulate your breathing when you do Yoga at your own time. You have to make sure you apply anything you would educate others.

There are surely many methods to teach others and apply things to your own life. For example, see how you apply teaching about your subject to learn more about a subject, from courses in your house to create an audio tape of yours simply.

## Exceptions to the Rule

This doesn't apply to every single individual every time, as with most things in life. For instance, it is said from my research that autistic persons are much more likely than attempting to educate or do it themselves via visual representations. I also know many folks who like audio rather than visuals, for example.

Furthermore, the cone numbers are used as a guideline, whereas some people are not as effective in learning by teaching others. Therefore, take a look at the most effective ones and try the ones that work best for you!

## HOW TO RECALL AN ENTIRE BOOK IN 5 MINUTES OR LESS

Have you ever read a brilliant book, and could you remember just one or two concepts after only a short period? It's incredibly aggravating — and it always occurs. But there is a technique not to forget what you read and to refresh it promptly if you do.

## Reading Goals, Cheated

The secret to properly reading is to participate in whatever you read. Underlining, asking, taking notes –are helpful, but you must know your aim if you want to read it efficiently. This is usual and a solid recommendation. But if you want to be successful and durable, you need more than a goal: a very real and detailed one.

Take a book like Getting Things Done, for example. The objective of "more organization" would be sufficient, but not only as a general aim. A generic aim can suffice to drive you to begin reading a book, but it will not be successful in reading the book. Something more specific is needed.

The difficulty is that after reading this, we only know the specifics of a book. So what should we do to set a specific objective in advance?

I thought one of the best targets while reading a book was to engage in creating a mental map of the text.

This is a particular objective for any book that you may utilize. Yes, it surely seems like cheating to be a "generic purpose specialized purpose," but you will not believe that it is so successful. It will assist in improving your understanding of reading; the greatest thing you can do is have a book summary that you can read at any moment. Unlike normal book synopsis, you may review it with lightning speed, very frequently at one glance, because of the special features of mind maps.

## TOP 3 BENEFITS OF MIND MAPPING A BOOK

### 1. Boost Comprehension While Reading

You will be 100% committed to reading, assured by a strong focus on generating such a specified deliverable such as a mental map.

In addition, you'll always be looking for and remembering what is already there every time you get to your mind map to add additional information. Indeed, it works so effectively that it generally takes months to refer again to the mental map.

## 2. Quickly Review the Entire Book Anytime

This is where mind mapping truly shines in comparison to other notes. What happens, months or even years after you have built a Mind Map, is fantastic. It is like the whole book being re-read in one look.

You did it actively when back first read this book, and merely scanning the mental map rapidly gives you all the book memories - even some you did not put in the map of your mind. In fact, brain relationships are so strong that you often feel the feelings that you had at the moment. And you don't actually need more than five minutes to check it with such a customised and concise summary.

## 3. Distill the Real Substance of the Book

Long novels that lead to tiny mind maps are not uncommon. The true content of the text is visible through building an intellectual map. Not all things in a book are right to the point: authors (validly) build up and develop crucial ideas with repeated stories and examples. You only need normal mind mapping to show this importance: use bold, write in larger letters or different colors your themes. With your custom mind map, you may reduce all fat while maintaining intact the relationships and the relative significance of each issue.

## Keep the Flow

Do not concurrently read and create the mind map to disturb the lecture flow. Instead, circle, emphasize the key themes and sentences for your summary and take notes as read. Not only does this intermediary step keep you in context and involved with the book, but it also makes it much easier to develop your mind map fast after reading the book's key portions. And you will get further strengthening of the material through this approach.

### Sleep on It

Just after reading the book, try not to work on your mind map. Instead, let your mind chew on what you read initially for some time. It's a nice thumb rule to do the next day. If you read this every day, work on your mental map for yesterday's topic before the reading session today is an excellent method of accomplishing it. In addition, try not to get your readings too far ahead of your mental mapping - if there is too much material to add in one sit, you will miss the advantages of repeat reinforcement and get overwhelmed.

### Use Dual Bookmarking

Use an additional bookmark rather than a single bookmark to identify the location of your book. Then, you don't have to worry about falling into your second bookmark while you read. I also propose that you use colorful Post-it flags.

### Try It

Will it does not take much longer than normal to read books using this method? Of course – but how is it that multiple books are published, with a bit of proportion of their material preserved – and only for a limited period?

You probably do – you won't push yourself to utilize it by all means if you merely read casually and think this strategy is over-killed. But if a fantastic book is in your hands – and so many are out – try mapping. Please try. You're not going to regret taking these additional efforts to keep your books going.

# WAYS TO BEAT DOWN STRESS BY DEVELOPING INNER PEACE

More, better, smarter, extra: Our world is growing rapidly and in recent years, it has evolved its dynamics. More swiftly than ever before, are economic and social forces altering. The daily lives of enterprises, employers, and organizations are growing more and more complex and for everyone: Our work is getting tougher, life is getting busier, and people around us are getting harder. Peace within - what's that?

And although we endeavor to be as efficient as possible, social networks advise that we also have to upload as many selfies and get hundreds of likes as feasible. In sum, we live in a fast-paced time when perpetual growth and required leisure seem to be impossible to combine. This causes a sensation of strain and pressure, through which we lose our inner core in the long term. But there is another way!

*For more inner peace: deceleration in everyday life*

Fortunately, many counter-movements form themselves in tandem, seeking quiet and restoration to inner harmony. Their shared purpose is slowing. Some of these social and cultural counter-movements are, for example, Slow Food, Cittàslow, Slowretail and Slow Travel. They are about patience, conscious awareness, consistency, sustainability, and thoughtful contact with yourself, fellow human beings, and the environment. The Slow movement is therefore meant to help restore balance to our hurried environment.

## TIPS FOR INNER PEACE

But you may also do a few things to slow down in modest ways. This doesn't mean that you should block out reality and wage war on the outside world. On the contrary: if you have found or restored your inner peace, you will be much more balanced, focused and effective in everyday life. You think more optimistically and feel more calm. Now you may find out the methods and behavioural recommendations you may employ to slow down and eventually reach inner calm.

### 1. control your thoughts

The major source of Stress is unwanted thoughts. Your brain helps you to tackle difficult issues, but at the same time, it fosters numerous new issues. Because restlessness, unbalance and unhappiness are typically the outcome of bad thinking. If you are troubled with thoughts about the future, concerns, self-doubt or feelings of guilt, it is difficult for you to let go and relax. Our brain doesn't discriminate between actual Stress and mental stress that exists only in your thoughts when you worry about something.

But fretting is utterly unneeded. Because the great majority of our anxieties never become true. And if they do occur, you build entirely different energy based on the scenario you don't even know yet. So why become upset before anything has happened? It merely costs you the energy that you might be utilizing for something far more worthwhile. Moreover, as soon as you become conscious of how crucial it is to manage your thoughts, you take a major step closer to your inner peace.

## 2. for inner peace: enjoy more consciously

Life is all about the simple moments. It's not about pursuing one highlight after the other, but about finding contentment in the daily. Perhaps you know moments in which you suddenly get a sense of happiness and fulfillment? This happens, for example, when the sunbeams warmly on your face on the way to work, you enjoy a good meal or treat yourself to a refreshing shower after a challenging workout.

Learn to capture these moments and be grateful for them. If you manage to appreciate the tiny everyday joys intentionally, you will inevitably slow down. Because in these moments you concentrate entirely on the beauty and allow yourself vital breaks and peaceful time out. Conscious enjoyment is medicine for your soul and a fantastic method to build inner serenity.

### 3. do not compare yourself

Comparing is human - and yet it increases your well-being in very few instances. Because there will always be someone who is more successful, brighter, more athletic or financially better positioned than you. On the other hand, as we all know, the grass is always greener. So even if you're merely comparing yourself to yourself (or a concept of yourself), you're not coming off very good. After all, there's always something you could modify.

Comparisons may place you in the 'if, then' trap mentally. It's like, "If I'm successful and climb the job ladder, then I'll be happy." Or, "If I'm financially secure, then I'm living a nice life." These ideas link to points in the future and motivate you. This in turn, creates pressure and acceleration. If, on the other hand, you wish to slow down and discover your inner calm, you should avoid needless comparisons and 'if, then statements.

### 4. meditate regularly

Another approach to actively slow down your ordinary life is meditation. Because during a Meditation, you focus on your inner self and leave the chaotic, fast-moving exterior for a brief while. There are many distinct styles of meditation. If you have not yet had any interaction with meditation, it is preferable to start with easy breathing exercises.

Take five minutes, inhale deeply and exhale comfortably. Concentrate entirely on your breath and let your thoughts flow without guiding them in any specific way. Embark on a journey to oneself. The more regularly you integrate these brief but intensive time-outs into your hectic regular life, the more relaxed and tranquil you will become.

### 5. develop an inner strength

He who has inner strength is psychologically strong, relaxes in himself and does not allow himself to be taken off track by anything or anybody. Hectic, worry and anxiety absolutely bounce off him and troubles on the outside do not influence his interior badly. But how can you get this extremely wonderful force, the inner strength? In any case, not from one day to the next.

It is a long process in which you must separate yourself from the views of others and stop comparing yourself. You must learn not to put your personal happiness reliant on other people or external events. And you should create a positive mentality to turn negative ideas and beliefs into positive ones. The good news is that you may have a pleasant state of mind and inner power may be gained and developed step by step. In this approach, you become mentally invincible and obtain inner serenity.

# POWERFUL METHODS FOR ENHANCING ATTENTION AND CONCENTRATION

In our digital age, we are easily sidetracked. Information is ubiquitous and we feel the need to deal with expanding and various sources of information. It draws on our time and our attention.

The inability to concentrate on the work at hand is one of the diseases of our time—everyone wants to know how to focus better and concentrate. Yet, the benefits of boosting attention and attention make it an issue worth addressing.

## What is concentration?

In Will Power & Self Discipline, Remez Sasson argued that focus is the power to direct one's attention following one's will. Concentration means control of attention. It is the ability to focus the mind on one subject, object, or concept, and at the same time eliminate from the mind any other unrelated thoughts, thoughts, feelings, and sensations.

That last step is the tough part for most of us. To concentrate is to eliminate, or not pay attention to, every other unrelated thought, idea, feeling, or experience. For example, to not pay attention to the numbers, beeps, and other signs that we have a new message, a new update, a new "like," a new follower!

Our everyday routine is governed by switching in and out of our mobile phones and computer. We get a steady flood of messages from WhatsApp, email, Telegram, and the half-dozen additional applications that are apparently vital to our profession. We continually hunt for knowledge to assist solve our everyday difficulties or get our work done.

Frequent interruptions hinder productivity. It takes longer to accomplish a task. We don't listen as well. We don't perceive things as well, whether with our spouse or with coworkers, and end up in misunderstanding, misinterpretation, and confrontation. It impairs memory. We forget things or can't recollect facts quickly, which impacts our personal lives and professional image.

## FACTORS AFFECTING CONCENTRATION

Some days it seems like our attention is under attack from all sides. In reality, concentration is impacted by both internal and external or environmental influences. If you want to learn how to enhance attention and memory, it helps to understand what's getting in the way today.

- **Distraction.** We are inundated with a steady flow of information, whether new or old, during the process of accomplishing anything. Researchers have revealed that our brains are so ready for this distraction that was simply seeing our smartphone hampers our ability to concentrate. We continually analyze whether knowledge is valuable, adequate, or meaningless. The sheer amount was pouring in muddles our judgement of whether we genuinely need additional information to make judgments.

- **Insufficient sleep.** Scientists have observed that lack of sleep can contribute to poorer attentiveness, slower mental processes, and impaired attention. You will have greater trouble focusing your attention and may feel confused. As a result, your ability to complete tasks notably linked to thinking or logic might be adversely damaged. Chronically bad sleep further impacts your focus and memory. Dr. Allison T. Siebern from the Stanford University Sleep Medicine Centre says that it is unlikely to make it to either your short- or long-term memory if you cannot concentrate on what is at hand.

- **Insufficient physical activity.** Have you ever noticed how strenuous exercise leaves you feeling more calm and energised throughout the day? However, when you don't conduct physical exercise, your muscles might get stiff. As a result, you may experience stiffness in your neck, shoulder, and chest and such prolonged, low-level discomfort might disrupt your attention.

- **Eating habits.** What we eat adds to how we feel, particularly our mental sharpness and clarity, throughout the day. If we don't nourish our brain with the right nutrients, we start to feel symptoms like memory loss, weariness, and lack of attention. For example, low-fat diets can damage attention since the brain needs specific critical fatty acids. Other restrictive diets may negatively affect attention by not giving the nutrients the brain requires or producing hunger, desires, or a sense of unwellness in the body that distracts itself.

- **Environment.** Depending on what you are doing, the surroundings might alter your attention. Obviously a noise level that is too high is an issue, but many individuals also have difficulties concentrating when it is too quiet. It isn't simply the total noise level, but the sort of noise that matters: the high-energy, nameless buzz of a coffee shop could inspire attention while the overheard chat of two co-workers derails it. A favorite song rapidly gets you singing along, delightfully distracted, whereas less distinguishing instrumentals could keep you alert to the work. Lighting that is too bright or too faint might damage your vision. A room that is too hot or too chilly generates pain.

All of these elements can impair your focus. But, happily, they are also all addressable.

## CONDITIONS RELATED TO CONCENTRATION

If you regularly can't focus your thoughts and are suffering continuous concentration challenges, it may suggest a cognitive, medical, psychological, lifestyle, or environmental problem. Depending on the cause, you may have to temporarily accept that your focus is poor and learn a few ways to decrease the impact or accept the dips as they happen. If you need help with focus and think your challenges go beyond the list above, contact with a specialist.

Cognitive. Your attention may drop if you find yourself forgetting things quickly. Your memory occasionally fails you. You misplace articles and have difficulties recalling things that occurred a short time ago. Another way your focus may be cognitively hampered is to discover that your mind is hyperactive, always thinking of several things due to concerns or essential occurrences. When ideas and concerns invade in your mind, demanding attention, it hampers good focus.

**Psychological.** When you are sad and feeling down, it is tough to focus. Similarly, when you are healing from the death of a loved one during mourning or are feeling worried, you may have difficulties focusing on a single job.

**Medical.** Medical disorders including diabetes, hormone abnormalities, and low red blood cell count might influence our focus. Some medicine also makes you drowsy or foggy and significantly impairs focus.

**Environment.** Poor working environments, shared areas, and strong or unfavorable work dynamics may also lead to lack of attention. For example, when we are facing burnout or stress from a job or personal life, we will find it difficult to concentrate due to emotional tiredness. Similarly, the environment may bring pain to our body with impacts that we're conscious of (hot, light, noise) and others that don't completely register (stress, negativity, monitoring). (tension, negativity, monitoring)..

**Lifestyle.** Fatigue, hunger, and dehydration can disrupt focus. In addition, lifestyles that entail too many missed meals, rich foods, or excessive alcohol intake might test our memory and capacity to concentrate and focus.

## WAYS TO IMPROVE YOUR CONCENTRATION

Now you realize why you need aid with concentration. What can assist you to focus better? There's no one answer for how to enhance attention, but the following suggestions can assist.

- **Eliminate distractions.** How do we focus better if we are continually overwhelmed with information? First, do a practice to reserve time in your calendar to complete a specific chore or activity. During this time, request that you be left alone or go to a place where others are unlikely to disturb you: a library, a coffee shop, a quiet room.

- Close social media and other apps, mute notifications, and keep your phone hidden from sight in a bag or backpack. As described in HBR, researchers showed that cognitive capability was considerably better when the phone was out of sight, not merely turned off. Keep Your major concentration is to do what you need to do. Shutting out both internal and external disruptions might assist you in concentrating.

- **Reduce multitasking.** Attempting to execute numerous tasks at the same time helps us feel productive. Unfortunately, it's also a formula for decreased attention, poor concentration, and decreased productivity. And lesser productivity can lead to burnout. Examples of multitasking include listening to a podcast while replying to an email or chatting to someone over the phone while writing your report. Such multitasking not only impairs your capacity to focus but lowers your job quality.

- **Practice mindfulness and meditation.** Meditating or practicing mindfulness exercises can boost well-being and mental fitness and increase attention. During the meditation process, our brain becomes quieter and our whole body gets more relaxed. We focus on our breath through the procedure so that we will not be sidetracked by our brains. With experience, we may learn to utilize our breath to bring our focus back to a particular job to be done properly, even if we get interrupted.

- **Get more sleep.** Many variables impact your sleep. One of the most prevalent is reading from an electronic device like a computer, phone, or tablet or viewing your favorite movie or TV show on an LED TV soon before night. Research has demonstrated that such gadgets emit light towards the blue end of the spectrum. Such light will excite your eye retina and impede the release of melatonin that promotes sleep anticipation in the brain. Use a filter or "blue light" glasses to limit such blue light or avoid all electronic gadgets before night. Other techniques to promote sleep include avoiding exertion late in the day, remaining hydrated throughout the day, employing journaling or breathing techniques to calm the mind, and developing a consistent nighttime routine and schedule.

- **Choose to focus on the moment.** It could feel contradictory when you cannot concentrate, but remember that you select where you focus. It's challenging to focus when your mind is continually in the past and thinking about the future. While it isn't easy, attempt to let go of previous experiences. Acknowledge the effect, what you felt, and what you learned from it, then let it go. Similarly, address your anxieties about the future, analyze how you are experiencing that worry in your body, then choose to let it go. We want to teach our mental resources to focus on the minutiae of what matters at present. Our brains travel in the direction we choose to focus.

- **Take a short break.** This, too could sound contradictory, but when you focus on anything for a long period, your attention may begin to wane down. As a result, you may feel more and more trouble paying your concentration to work.

- Researchers have shown that our brains tend to overlook sources of continual stimulus. Taking extremely brief pauses by diverting your attention elsewhere can substantially increase mental concentration after that. The next time you are working on a project, take a break when you begin to feel stuck. Move about, chat to someone, or even move to a new sort of activity. You will return back with a more concentrated mind to maintain your performance high.

- **Connect with nature.** Research has showed that simply having plants in office spaces may aid enhance attention and productivity and job happiness and improved air quality. In addition, finding time to take a stroll in the park or enjoying the plants or flowers in your yard will enhance your concentration and help you feel rejuvenated.

- **Train your brain.** Scientific research is starting to gather data on the capacity of brain training exercises to boost cognitive capacities, particularly focus, in adults. Such brain training games may also help you enhance your working and short-term memory, as well as your processing and problem-solving skills. Examples of such games include jigsaw puzzles, sudoku, chess, and brain-stimulating video games.

- **Exercise.** Start your day with a basic workout and get your body moving. According to the May 2013 issue of the Harvard Men's Health Watch, daily exercise produces chemicals crucial for memory, focus, and mental sharpness. Other studies indicated that exercise could raise the brain's dopamine, norepinephrine, and serotonin levels, influencing concentration and attention. Individuals who engage in some type of exercise or sports do better on cognitive tests than individuals who have poor physical health. In addition, physical activity helps relax the muscles and reduce stress in the body. Since the body and mind are so tightly linked, when your body feels better, so, too, will your mind.

- **Listen to music.** Music has been found to have healing benefits for our brains. Light music may allow you to concentrate better, yet certain music may distract you. Experts usually agree that classical music and environmental sounds, such as water running, are ideal alternatives for focus, whereas music with lyrics and human voices may be distracting. Multiple applications and services offer background music and soundscapes suited for different sorts of attention and work demands.

- **Eat well.** Choose foods that control blood sugar, sustain energy, and fuel the brain. Fruits, vegetables, and rich fiber diets may keep your blood sugar levels equal. Reduce sugary meals and drinks that create spikes and dips in blood sugar levels that make you feel dizzy or tired.

- Your brain requires loads of healthy fat to function correctly. Nuts, berries, avocados, and coconut oil are all fantastic ways to add healthy fats into your diet and help your brain work more smoothly. The science of Research has revealed that fruits like blueberries can enhance concentration and memory for up to 5 hours after intake due to an enzyme that boosts the flow of oxygen and blood to the brain, assisting with memory and our capacity to focus and acquire new information. In addition, leafy green foods such as spinach include potassium, increasing the connections between neurons and making our brain more receptive.

- **Set a daily priority.** Write out what you want to do each day, ideally the night before, and choose a single objective that you commit to fulfilling. This will help focus your thinking on what counts, do the important chores first, and leave the trivial stuff for later. Break enormous jobs into smaller chunks so that you will not be overwhelmed. Identifying actual objectives can help decrease distracting worry, and attaining tiny daily goals helps train your brain to accomplish success.

- **Create space for work.** Create a tranquil, dedicated location for work, if feasible. Not everyone can have a well-appointed workplace, but desk organizers, noise-canceling headphones, an adjustable display, and adjustable lighting can assist. Clear clutter out of sight, make it as ergonomic and pleasant as possible and attempt to maintain your environment tidy and aired.

- **Use a timer.** Train your brain to hyper-focus on a task by utilizing a timer or phone alarm. First, identify what work you wish to do. Set your timer for 20 minutes (usually not more than 30 minutes) and concentrate on the job. When the alarm chimes, take a small rest for 5 minutes. You may either take a stroll, perform some stretching exercise, reset the timer, and start again. This strategy has been demonstrated to be useful to boost your concentration.

- **Switch tasks**. While we may wish to concentrate on a specific subject, sometimes we become stuck and our brain needs something fresh to focus on. Try moving to other duties or something you enjoy doing. Switching tasks might help you stay awake and productive for a longer duration.

Learning how to enhance focus is not something you can acquire immediately. Professional sportsmen like golfers, sprinters, gymnasts require a lot of time to train (and typically have a coach) to concentrate and get the perfect move at the right moment to attain perfection.

The first step to enhance your focus is to realize how it is influencing your life. For example, suppose you are failing to meet obligations, continuously diverted by the irrelevant, or not progressing toward your objectives. In that case, it is time to seek help with concentration so that you can focus on what matters most to you.

Learning how to concentrate at work is vital for excelling in your profession and life. By enhancing your focus, you will find that you can do more of what you value and feel better doing it. It's not only about achieving chores but about making time for joy and pleasure so that you may create a meaningful and rewarding existence.

# RETAINING INFORMATION TO IMPROVE YOUR CIRCUMSTANCES

Learning is the input for growth and works as a fundamental component of life. If you want to experience progress in all directions, then you need to invest in learning tactics.

However, learning requires time, and time is a scarce thing. So, how can you maximize your time by learning and remembering knowledge fast?

*Here are 12 effective sorts of learning tactics that may extend your perspective and help you keep information at rapid speed.*

## 1. HONE YOUR NOTE-TAKING SKILLS

I have found out that the old-fashioned technique of taking notes is more productive than entering your notes on the sticky notes given by your gadget. So, if you want to study quicker, ignore the laptop and use your pen and paper to take notes. Research found that students who use paper and pen to take notes in class remember more information than those who type their lecture notes on a laptop.

Writing abilities involve different regions of your brain than reading. When you spend time writing thoughts in your notepad, having examined the information, you will have more opportunity to address the subject again. This will fascinate visual learners while the auditory learners can read the text loudly in addition to writing it down.

While it may be difficult and longer to take notes by hand instead than typing, writing increases retention and understanding. You keep knowledge longer in your memory when you write with your hand, which implies you can swiftly recall knowledge and do better during an examination.

Quality notes assist faster learning. Developing the power of taking excellent notes can enable you to grasp concepts and fully comprehend the topic matter. Therefore, it is best to acquire note-taking skills and tactics before you acquire a new topic.

This ability will allow you to arrange your lecture notes into consumable portions. For instance, if you are participating in an online course, don't just observe, and do the following:

- Listen, summarize the knowledge gained and then take notes.
- Create lines and spaces between the main concepts so you can add more info subsequently during revision.
- Use symbols and abbreviations to save time.
- Write in phrases instead of complete sentences.
- Pull out the necessarv info and neglect the trivial ones.

## 2. Study, Sleep and Study More

Do you have a crucial presentation, but you were unable to find time to prepare?

Most persons who find themselves in this circumstance would prefer to remain overnight and cram before the presentation. The wonderful part is the hard effort will undoubtedly be paid even if you are fatigued the following day. However, that's not the most effective amongst many learning ways to remember knowledge swiftly.

Research suggests that there is a linkage between sleep and learning. Sleep promotes learning by enhancing your attention. You cannot focus if you deprive yourself of quality sleep. Not only that, but sleep also increases memory consolidation, which is critical for learning.

Getting some sleep strengthens your brain to recall rapidly.

Deep sleep before learning new knowledge might boost memory. If you study and get some shut-eye, you will not only be able to explore more, but you will accomplish peak performance in your learning experience—a good example of learning tactics for students.

### 3. Tweak Your Learning Strategies & Processes

Someone argues you cannot repeat the same method and obtain a different outcome. However, making some alterations in recurrent practice classes can allow you to learn a new ability faster instead of keeping to a routine.

You can learn a skill by watching YouTube videos, play games, or read a guide in a textbook. Another comparable example is adjusting the size of your racket when honing your lawn tennis game.

### 4. Use a Mnemonic Strategy

The mnemonic approach is one of the time-tested learning methodologies. You can learn anything faster by employing a mnemonic strategy – sounds, letter patterns, or other approaches that assist you to memorize an idea. This was quite popular in kindergarten to learn the alphabet. Children may 'know their ABCs' owing to the alphabet song and retain this information.

Mnemonics will assist you to condense, simplify, and condense the knowledge so it can be simpler to keep. This learning approach is excellent for medical or legal students or anyone studying a language.

So, if you want to keep considerable material, adopt a mnemonic strategy, and you will realize you can recall material beyond your examination.

### 5. DISCOVER YOUR PEAK MOMENT WHEN YOU ARE THE MOST ATTENTIVE AND ALERT

You have intense attention during a precise hour during the day, which varies from person to person. Some are early risers, while others are night owls.

Discovering your individuality will aid you in knowing what times of the day you can remember knowledge faster.

### 6. Focus on Topics One After the Other

Some topics demand an additional level of focus to understand properly. Jumping from one issue to the next might make your efforts unproductive, which will hinder you in keeping the material. This arises from key learning tactics for pupils to help them study more efficiently.

### 7. Pause

We constantly desire to hurry through content while we are reading. The effect is obvious-limited retention.

Absorb material in little chunks, pause to ponder on what you have read, review the thought, then go.

### 8. Make it Pleasurable

If you are challenging to understand a topic, personalize it. You may accomplish this by finding out how it connects to your personal life or profession.

### 9. Utilize Brain Breaks to Regain Focus

Information overload is real. Do you know that your brain needs to convey messages to your sensory receptors to store new information?

Your brain instinctively shuts down when you are nervous, perplexed, or overwhelmed. You might detect this among learners during a long lecture. They will cease paying attention to what's being taught.

One of the finest learning ways to overcome this is to go on a 'brain break' or redirect your focus to something new. For example, you may view a five-minute motivational movie to clear your thoughts or do something that fascinates you.

### 10. Stay Hydrated

You have read that water is excellent for your body system and skin. It enhances your bodily functioning and enhances your immune system. Now being hydrated also affects your cognitive functioning favorably. So you can get smarter when you drink water.

A study found out that pupils who took water to the test hall scored better than those who did not.

### 11. Link What You Learn with Previous Knowledge

You will comprehend new knowledge faster if you link new concepts with an old thought you already know. However, in the book, Make it Stick, the authors argued that linked study habits are most often unhelpful. They may produce an appearance of grasp and mastery, but the knowledge slips away from our memory fast.

Memory is vital when performing challenging cognitive activities, including applying the information to new activities and drawing conclusions from already known information or facts. By uncovering the techniques of connecting new information with existing experience, you will find more levels of comprehension in the new topic. This will help you learn quicker and retain knowledge at lightning speed.

Guess who enjoys utilizing this learning strategy? Elon Musk, the creator of SpaceX and Tesla. Elon compares knowledge to a semantic tree. He suggests ensuring you know the basics — the trunk and the branches before digging into the foliage or details. That way, you will discover something to latch on to. Then, you give the mental hook when you relate new information to the old.

## 12. Teach Learning Strategies to Others

If you find it tough to express a notion to others, you might also find it tough to retain the notion. Studies have found out that the average human recalls 90 percent of what was learned only when they educate others or execute the notion immediately. So you might uncover your weak spots when you implement or teach an idea.

Do you wish to retain info faster? Then, reread the content until you grow confident enough to share that piece of information with others.

*Bottom Line*

Great learners are still learning how to learn. Since learning is a lifelong affair, find the learning tactics that work for you. For example, don't attempt to speed through a notion, understand the easy ideas, and build on the past knowledge when taking larger topics. The more you practice those learning tactics, the better you become at becoming a great learner.

# STEPS TO MEDITATE FOR LIFE-AFFIRMING ROUTINE

How do you learn to meditate? In mindfulness meditation, we learn how to pay attention to the breath as it goes in and out and notice when the mind wanders from this work. This practice of returning to the breath trains the muscles of attention and awareness.

When we pay attention to our breath, we are learning how to return to, and remain in, the present moment—to anchor ourselves in the here and now on purpose, without judgement.

The theory of mindfulness appears simple—the practice takes patience. Indeed, noted meditation instructor Sharon Salzberg relates that her first experience with meditation taught her how fast the mind gets caught up in other pursuits. "I thought, alright, what would it be, like, 800 breaths before my mind starts to wander? And to my great shock, it was one breath, and I'd be gone," recalls Salzberg.

## WHY LEARN TO MEDITATE?

A collection of benefits that are related to meditation.

While meditation isn't a cure-all, it may surely bring some much-needed space in your life. Sometimes, that's all we need to make better choices for ourselves, our families, and our communities. And the most crucial tools you can bring with you to your meditation practice are a little patience, some kindness for yourself, and a comfortable spot to sit.

When we meditate, we infuse far-reaching and long-lasting advantages into our lives. And bonus: you don't need any extra gear or a pricey membership.

*Here are five reasons to meditate:*

- Understanding your pain
- Lower your stress
- Connect better|
- Improve focus
- Reduce brain chatter

## HOW TO MEDITATE

Meditation is something everyone can do, here's how.

Meditation is easy (and harder) than most people imagine. So read these instructions, make sure you're somewhere where you can relax into this process, set a timer, and give it a shot:

1) Take a seat

Find a spot to sit that seems serene and peaceful to you.

2) Set a time limit

If you're just beginning, it might assist in setting a small duration, such as five or 10 minutes.

3) Notice your body

You can sit in a chair with your feet on the floor, you can sit freely cross-legged, you may kneel—all are good. Just make sure you are steady and in a position, you can stay in for a while.

4) Feel your breath

Follow the feel of your breath as it goes in and as it goes out.

5) Notice when your mind has wandered

Inevitably, your focus will leave the breath and move to other locations. When you come around to detecting that your mind has wandered—in a few seconds, a minute, five minutes—

simply restore your focus to the breath.

6) Be kind to your wandering mind

Don't condemn yourself or stress about the content of the ideas you find yourself caught in. Just come back.

7) Close with kindness

When you're ready, softly elevate your gaze (if your eyes are closed, open them) (if your eyes are closed, open them). Take a minute and observe any noises in the surrounding. Notice how your body feels right now. Notice your ideas and feelings.

That's it! That's the practice. You go away, you come back, and you try to do it as politely as possible.

## How Much Should I Meditate?

Meditation is no more complicated than what we've detailed before. It is that easy … and that tough. But, it's also strong and worth it. The goal is to resolve to sit every day, even if it's for five minutes. Meditation instructor Sharon Salzberg says: "One of my meditation instructors remarked that the most crucial moment in your meditation practice is the time you sit down to do it. Because right then, you're declaring to yourself that you believe in change, you believe in caring for yourself, and you're making it true. You're not simply retaining a value like mindfulness or compassion in the abstract, but genuinely making it real."

## MEDITATION TIPS AND TECHNIQUES

We've gone over the basic breath meditation so far. Still, other mindfulness techniques use different focal points than the breath to anchor our attention—external objects like a sound in the room, or something broader, such as noticing spontaneous things that come into your awareness during an aimless wandering practice. But all of these techniques have one thing in common: We realize that our thoughts ARE controlling the show a lot of the time. It's true. We think things normally, and then we act. But here are some useful ideas to shake it up:

### HOW TO MAKE MINDFULNESS A HABIT

It's believed that 95 percent of our behavior operates on autopilot. That's because brain networks underpin all of our habits, lowering our millions of sensory inputs each second into manageable shortcuts so we can operate in this chaotic world. Unfortunately, these default brain messages are so effective that they often drive us to relapse into previous behaviors before we recall what we planned to do instead.

Mindfulness is the exact opposite of these default processes. It's executive control rather than autopilot and permits conscious acts, volition, and decisions. But that requires practice. The more we exercise the intentional brain, the stronger it grows. Every time we do something purposeful and novel, we trigger neuroplasticity, stimulating our grey matter, which is full of newly sprung neurons that have not yet been groomed for "autopilot" brain.

But here's the problem. While our conscious brain understands what is best for us, our autopilot brain causes us to shortcut our way through life. So how do we prompt ourselves to be attentive when we need it most? This is where the idea of "behavior design" enters in. It's a method to put your deliberate brain in the driver's seat. There are two methods to achieve that—first, slowing down the autopilot brain by putting hurdles in its way, and second, eliminating barriers in the route of the purposeful brain so that it can seize control.

Shifting the balance to give your purposeful brain greater power requires some work, though. Here are some methods to get started.

- **Put meditation reminders around you.** If you want to practice some yoga or to meditate, put your yoga mat or your meditation cushion in the middle of your floor so you can't miss it as you go by.

- **Refresh your reminders regularly.** Say you decide to use sticky notes to remind yourself of a new aim. That could work for about a week, but then your autopilot brain and old patterns take over again. Try composing new notes to yourself; add variety or make them amusing. That way, they'll remain with you longer.

- **Create new patterns.** You may use a sequence of "If this, then that" messages to generate easy reminders to shift into the purposeful brain. For instance, you may come up with, "If office door, then deep breath," as a method to transition into mindfulness as you are about to start your workday. Or, "If phone calls, take a breath before answering." Each purposeful activity to transition into mindfulness will build your purposeful brain.

# CONCLUSION

If you want to learn, do the genuine thing. Everybody learns what their profession demands them to memorize, what it enables them to reference, and when it's better to consult with an expert. The memorizing you'll complete through performing the task, not establishing a memory palace.

School is a signalling system. The wise thing to do is focus on optimizing your grades with the least effort, not memorizing your gen chem textbook. Real learning is what you do on the job. So you should focus all your efforts on achieving the job you desire as efficiently as possible, not on this self-gratifying scholasticism. If you're getting tested on your calculations and admitted to grad school or employed based on your marks, then forget deep learning - start grinding!

I'm hoping the grind-and-graduate attitude is not just depressing but also suboptimal. It could be that memory palaces can be not simply a sluggish and colorful hard drive but can also allow you to undertake creative thinking, build up mathematical methods, and broaden what you're able to learn.

It'll be hard to say what's achievable without a lot more practice. But I've never heard any instructor provide one ounce of instruction on any of this in my life, which makes me think it's definitely a neglected area. Visual thinking aptitude and creativity are hard to assess even by the norms of psychology and education research, and it's hard to develop into a product. So no wonder. I believe it would be good just to have some case studies from folks in our community who are ready to try it and see what occurs.

**Do Not Go Yet; One Last Thing To Do**

If you liked this book or found it useful, I'd appreciate it if you could leave a quick review on Amazon. Your support is greatly appreciated, and I personally read all of the reviews in order to obtain your feedback and improve the book.

*Thanks for your help and support!*

Printed in Great Britain
by Amazon

65152899R00111